FOAM DÉCOR

KRISTY McNEIL

745.593 M2332
McNeil, Kirsty.
Foam d´ecor

AUG 2 1 2003

MID-CONTINENT PUBLIC LIBRARY
Kearney Branch
100 S. Platte-Clay Way
Kearney, Mo. 64060

KE

WITHDRAW
from records of
Mid-Continent Public Library

D1365821

©2003 Kristy McNeil

Published by

700 East State Street • Iola, WI 54990-0001
715-445-2214 • 888-457-2873
www.krause.com

Please call or write for our free catalog of publications. Our toll-free number to place an order or obtain a free catalog is 800-258-0929, or please use our regular business telephone 715-445-2214.

All rights reserved. No portion of this publication may be reproduced or transmitted in any form or by any means, electronic or mechanical, including photocopy, recording, or any information storage and retrieval system, without permission in writing from the publisher, except by a reviewer who may quote brief passages in a critical article or review to be printed in a magazine or newspaper, or electronically transmitted on radio or television.

All photography by Tony Frederick, unless otherwise noted.
Step out photos by Kristy McNeil
Edited by Jodi Frazzell
Designed by Marilyn McGrane

Library of Congress Catalog Number: 2002113143

ISBN: 0-87349-606-X

Acknowledgments

As I began the adventure that has brought my ideas to all of you, there were people without whom I could not have accomplished this monumental task! Thank you Jeremy and Nathan for your support and patience. I also would like to thank Melissa Kirkman, Wendy Foster and Kalyn Smith for jumping in when needed. To my mother and partner in creativity, Denise Russell, thank you does not even begin to cover it! Thanks for your babysitting, proofreading, and for the countless hours of hard work! Dad, thank you for all of the late night prep hours!

Finally, thanks to all of the wonderful Krause family! Don and Jodi, I really appreciate your patience and support. Special thanks also go to photographer, Tony Frederick, for your tremendous talents.

Table of Contents

MID-CONTINENT PUBLIC LIBRARY

3 0000 12405107 3

MID-CONTINENT PUBLIC LIBRARY
Kearney Branch
100 S. Platte-Clay Way
Kearney, Mo. 64060

KE

INTRODUCTION

CHAPTER 1: TOOLS AND MATERIALS

CHAPTER 2: ARCHITECTURAL ELEGANCE

23 Gothic Floral Plaque
24 Medieval Ornamental Plaque
26 Gothic Face Oil Lamp
28 Medieval Carved Shelf
30 French Scroll Sconce
32 Scroll Finial
33 German Scrollwork Cornice
35 French Ironwork Planter
38 Fanlight Votive
41 Filigree Accent Lamp
43 Oval Cartouche
45 Victorian Silhouette
46 Rusted Key and Key Plate
49 Flared Box Clock
53 Fleur-de-Lis Medallion
54 Doorway Arch
57 *Gallery*

CHAPTER 3: CONTEMPORARY FLAIR

Suspended Art 62
Deco Influence Console Table 65
Wavy Wall Sconce 67
Sunburst Curtain Rod Finial 68
Illuminated Frames 71
Gallery 73

CHAPTER 4: GARDEN GATHERING

76 Whimsical Sundial
79 Stamped Ornament
80 Scroll Ornament
82 Garden Party Lights
84 Weathered Crackle Window
86 Garden Statue
87 Garden Finial
88 Bird Bath and Feeder
90 Flared Box Planter
92 Fabulous Floor Fountain
95 *Gallery*

RESOURCES

Welcome to Foam Décor!

You are about to embark on a creative journey that is going to awaken ideas you never knew were there! In the age of reproduction antiques, I thought it would be great to make my own treasures. I decided to see what I could do with craft foam and have developed the concept into *Foam Décor*. Today, we want to be surrounded by antiquity, but many of us cannot afford to invest in reproductions, not to mention the actual antiques. *Foam Décor* allows you to create elegant surroundings with very little money.

Another thing that prompted me to create *Foam Décor* is the fact that I do not have a salvage yard in my area. So many times our favorite television shows send us to salvage yards to find fabulous finds, but some of us have no place to go! Even if you do have someplace in your area, perhaps you do not have the time to dig around, haggle, and then clean up that wonderful bargain.

Foam Décor is empowering. You will feel at ease creating new projects because you are only working with foam. It is easily and inexpensively replaced. Since foam is easily cut, it makes learning how to use tools simple! I hope you will feel a tremendous amount of gratification once you complete these projects.

So let's get started! Although the entire book may be completed by nearly any skill level, I have color coded the projects to help ease you into the various techniques. Have fun! And relax...it is only foam!

COLOR KEY

Level 1	Level 2	Level 3

Chapter 1

Tools and Techniques

There are three steps to creating foam décor: cutting (and/or carving), covering (the foam), and finishing (faux painting). One of the greatest things about creating foam décor is that getting started does not require a huge monetary investment. You may choose to use the simple hand tools shown, or invest in the rotary and heated tools. Please keep in mind that the rotary and heated tools will save a lot of time if you plan to try many of the projects throughout the book. Throughout this book, I will list the most time saving tool(s) in each materials list.

Types of Foam

Foam Décor projects may be composed of any type of foam! If it is foam, consider using it. Several types of foam options are pictured.

There are a number of shapes and sizes of craft foam.

Basement insulation foam is another foam décor option. It is similar to packaging foam.

Exterior insulation foam is excellent for large-scale projects.

This flexible foam on a roll is normally used to insulate sills.

Kid's craft foam can work in some cases. However, keep in mind that you cannot easily cover it with joint compound. It is too thin and flexible for the projects in this book.

Even foam cups can be made into elegant creations. We will use these to make garden lighting. Not only can you punch designs into them, but you can also create wonderful embossed designs by simply drawing on these cups with a pen!

Cutting Tools

When cutting through craft foam, use your imagination. An obvious choice may be a kitchen knife. Some less obvious, but still simple to use, tools include a coping saw or a creative heat tool.

Use small-tooth knives from the kitchen or purchase a foam knife from the craft store.

Use a PVC pipe saw for long straight cuts.

A pull saw is a good alternative to a coping saw. The lightweight flexible blade works around curves nicely. Try both tools and decide which is most comfortable for you.

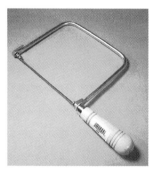

Left: The coping saw is a classic tool used to cut curving shapes and to get through thick pieces of foam. **Below:** A jigsaw saves time and gives the cleanest cuts. It can be used to do inside cutwork and just to cut through thick foam.

■ SERRATED KNIFE

The best knives for cutting foam have small teeth. Find them in your kitchen or at craft and home improvement stores.

■ PVC PIPE SAW

This tool is typically used to cut PVC pipe. It has small teeth, making it excellent for foam. Smaller teeth on a cutting tool create a smoother cut. We will use this tool to score long, straight lines with the aid of a ruler. This saw is also great for cutting away large areas quickly. While using the pipe saw, make single cuts to score the foam, then gently break it over the table edge.

■ PULL SAW

This tool is found at home stores and has a flexible blade. You may use this saw in place of a coping saw. Try the various cutting tools to see what you feel most comfortable with.

■ COPING SAW

The coping saw is great for cutting curved shapes through 1" to 2" thick foam. A disadvantage of this tool is that it can only be used to cut around the outer edges of a piece. This tool is easy to use. Just be sure to cut in an up and down motion versus allowing the blade to lean.

■ JIGSAW

A jigsaw is a true timesaver once you get used to the speed. It may be used when a coping saw is called for. This tool is wonderful for thick foam, up to 2". Not only can it cut the outside shapes from straight to curvy, but it can also be used to cut inside the foam such as in the Weathered Crackle Window located in the last project chapter. Be sure to choose a blade that has small teeth and is long enough to poke through the back of your foam piece.

To work with the jigsaw, always keep the tool over the edge of the worktable. You do not want to cut the table! Insert the blade through the foam. You do not need to turn on the saw yet. Next, press the trigger and let the blade work through the foam. The key to getting the smoothest cuts is to hold the foam steady on the work surface. Be sure to always hold the blade upright. This is easily accomplished by holding the foot of the tool flat on the foam. Always keep an eye ahead for where the blade needs to go next. Keep your hands away from the blade at all times. A jigsaw does not turn sharp corners. Continue around the corners just to cut away the bulk of the foam. Next, go back after the large area is cut away and cut toward the corner from one direction, then the other.

■ HOT MULTI-TIPPED TOOL

Look for a tool that comes with interchangeable tips. For foam projects, look specifically for a knife blade tip and a straight tip (soldering tip). When plugged in, the tool heats up to several hundred degrees. The heat enables the tips to glide through craft foam. Most often, you will use this tool on 1/2" thick craft foam sheets, but it can be used to score 1" thick material. You may also to use this tool for soldering, wood burning, and more! It has become indispensable to me when working on foam décor.

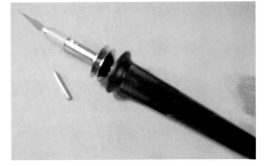

Become a foam cutting pro in no time! Keep these tips in mind when using the heat tool.

The heat tool is the most valuable tool if you plan to do a lot of foam décor projects. The heat allows the bits to glide through foam. The knife blade and straight blunt tip are used most often.

For ½" thick foam:

It is helpful to raise the sheet of foam by placing it on blocks. This will enable you to glide through the foam with ease while protecting your work surface. Position the blocks so that the area to be cut is between them. The blocks will help support the foam.

Practice cutting on the scrap areas of the sheet of foam. Cut straight through the foam rather than allowing the tool to tip at a 45° angle like a pencil. Notice how the foam continues to burn slightly after the blade passes through. Keep this in mind when cutting.

Do not try to cut tight areas in one pass of the blade. Glide the blade through one side, then re-insert from another angle to make the cut.

Take care when cutting around the outside. The piece will become somewhat fragile. If you happen to break the foam, it is easily fixed with a little glue and a toothpick. Break the toothpick in half. Dip it in glue and insert the glued end into one side of the foam to be joined. Apply glue to the other end of the toothpick and attach the other piece of foam. Your repair will be disguised in the finishing stages!

If you cut too fast, foam will build up on the blade and this will cause it to drag and catch on the foam, creating rough cuts. Pull the blade out of the foam and scrape away the buildup with a knife. Continue cutting a bit slower.

For cutting 1" thick foam:

All of the previous tips apply to cutting the thicker foam except the blade will not go completely through the back of the foam.

To get the complete cut you may do either of the following. Cut through the foam as far as the blade will go to score the piece, then carefully break the foam along the line. Or, score through the first side, then measure the line again and cut through the backside with the knife. The cuts should meet. Use the method you feel comfortable with.

Almost always, you will find that my projects use 1" thick foam to build structures such as boxes rather than scrolling designs. If you ever want a thicker scrolling design (like a cornice), I suggest cutting two of the design from the ½" thick foam and then gluing those together.

SAFETY FIRST!
- Keep pliers handy when working with the heat tool. The tip needs to be retightened periodically.
- Use goggles and a fume mask when working with the heated knife. The fumes are harmless, but can be irritating.
- To minimize strain on your wrist, small lightweight craft hammers and rubber mallets are best. These are also very inexpensive.
- Be sure sit the heat tool on a proper stand. It gets very hot!

To cut foam:

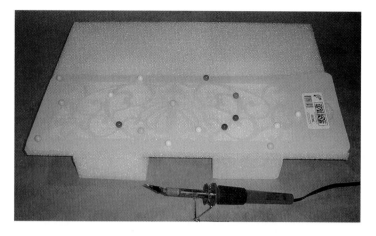

1. Pin the pattern to the foam with ball-tip pins. Elevate the foam on two blocks or scrap foam. Keep the area being cut between the two scrap pieces of foam for support. Move the blocks as needed.

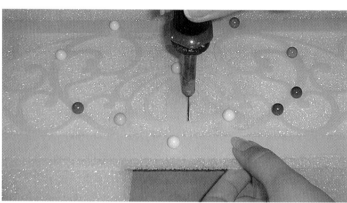

2. Cut around the pattern. Pierce all the way through the back of the foam. Keep the blade vertical when cutting. The blade tip may loosen while cutting. Keep pliers handy to tighten the tip when necessary. Take your time when cutting to prevent the blade from getting caught in the foam.

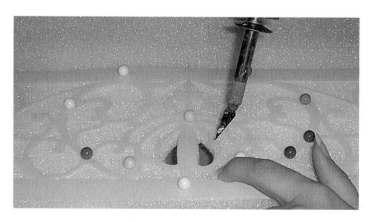

3. Gently poke the cut pieces through the back of the foam. They should go through easily. If not, reinsert the blade where the piece is stuck.

4. Continue to cut around the pattern to get the finished piece. This piece is ready to be covered.

Carving Tools

Carving tools are used to create relief, or carved details, on craft foam. These tools will not be used to carve all the way through the foam, but will remove portions from a thick piece. One example of a carved relief project is the Medieval Shelf (page 28).

■ POTATO PEELER

The potato peeler was the first carving tool I used. The types that do not have the plastic piece on the tip are best. This tool can be used in most any simplistic carving. Use the potato peeler to gouge away chinks of foam and to define where areas of foam need to be removed. This tool may be used in place of a rotary tool. However, it will take more time to finish the project.

A potato peeler is an excellent start for carving foam. It may be used to dig deep and remove foam during the relief craving process.

■ PENCIL OR PEN

A standard pencil is great for tracing patterns or scoring thin lines onto the foam. It is not good for carving large areas. A pen may also be used.

■ TRADITIONAL WOOD TOOLS

Traditional woodcarving tools work great on foam. These are a step up from using a potato peeler because of the comfort the handles afford and the various types available. If you are looking to purchase tools just for foam carving, I suggest the rotary tool. However, if you are absolutely afraid to try the power tool, a good set of traditional woodcarving tools are for you. Use them when the rotary tool is suggested.

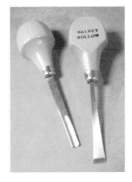

Traditional wood carving tools.

■ ECONOMY WOOD TOOLS

These usually come in a set. When I do use these, I use the flat tip, rounded tip, and the gouge tip. The gouge tip is the only one with a curved channel. These work fine on smaller projects (such as the 8" plaques, pages 23 and 24), but they are not very comfortable for large ones like the Medieval Shelf. The flat and rounded tip tools are used to cut through the foam. The gouge is used to tear away pieces. Economy wood tools are just what the names says—an affordable alternative. Once again, I prefer to use the rotary and heat tools to any of the hand tools.

■ YOUR HANDS

That is right! Since craft foam is easily cut, it is also easily torn away. After you use your favorite carving tool to define the outside edges of a carved area, you may simply tear away excess foam. You will need to smooth out the torn areas later, but this still saves time.

Economy wood carving tools.

■ ROTARY TOOL

A rotary tool spins at a very high speed. It is used for a variety of hobby and household jobs. Hundreds of bits are available to accommodate the task. However, we will concentrate on just a few.

One great advantage of this tool is that the bits do not wear down, so they are a one-time investment. The foam is so easy to get through, there is little resistance.

There are a number of rotary tools with many features. A less expensive model with variable speeds will be fine for your foam décor projects.

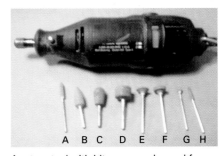

A rotary tool with bits commonly used for foam décor projects.

To use the rotary tool:

1. Pin the pattern to the foam. Here, flat-head straight pins have been inserted into the white areas of the pattern.

Bits

A B C D E F G H

2. Score the pattern into the foam with a small, pointed bit such as A or H (above, right). Drive the bit right through the pattern. Trace over all the black lines and around the edges of the large, black areas.

3. Peel away the large black areas left after scoring the pattern. You may leave the white areas of the pattern for now. Continue to carve the scored areas to about ½" depth with the same bit you have been using.

4. Start to carve the large open areas (where you peeled away the black pieces of pattern) to about ½" depth. Use a potato peeler (or just your hands) to tear away some of the excess foam.

5. Use a rounded or flat bottom bit (such as C or D) to deepen and smooth the torn areas. Hold the tool vertically and apply gentle pressure to get the bottom of the carved area leveled.

6. Bevel the edges of the carving to add dimension. Switch to a cone shaped bit (such as B). Hold tool so that side of the bit hits the foam. Run the bit along all of sides of the carved areas.

7. Add the final touches. Use small bits (such as A, F, G and H) to finish cleaning up any tight areas you may have missed or need deepening. This piece is ready to be covered.

Covering Foam

Once the foam is cut or carved, it must be beautified and strengthened by covering it. The final use for the object (whether it will be placed indoors or out) dictates which covering material you should use. Following are a few applicators used for foam décor creations.

Tip: Keep in mind that if you will be using a brush-on type of paint (NOT most spray paints) that the insides of small holes and tight areas will not have to be covered extensively with any covering material (just use the paint) nor does the back or bottom of most projects need to be treated. Be your own judge on how much to cover. If you cannot see the holes in tight areas, then use this tip.

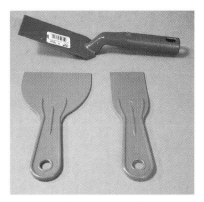

Applicators for large areas. These are referred to as putty knives in the book.

Indoor-Use Projects

If the project will stay indoors and will not come in contact with water, I have two favorite products to use. Joint compound is most often used. It is available at home stores and comes pre-mixed in a bucket. An all-purpose type can be used on any size project and is extremely economical. Joint compound may be textured in infinite ways, yet it can be sanded perfectly smooth, if desired.

Foam Finish™ (available at craft stores) is another great product. I used this one mostly for smaller projects, especially when I wanted a smooth final texture. This product is self-leveling, which saves sanding time. The only downfall is that it is not as economical as joint compound.

You may also use plaster of Paris, but beware. It will set up super fast! If you want the project to dry fast, then this is the product for you. Be sure to mix small amounts, because it literally takes less than 10 minutes for the product to become difficult to work with. It will not be as easy as the other products to sand after it hardens.

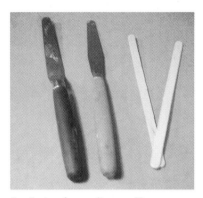

Applicators for small areas. These are referred to as pallet knives and craft sticks throughout the book. Round or flat shaped paint brushes may also be used.

Outdoor-Use Projects

Foam décor projects that will be used outdoors in the open need waterproofing. The faux finish also needs to be created with exterior paint, or a clear waterproofing sealer must be applied. To cover the foam in these cases, you have several options. Tile grout is preferred for objects that will stay outdoors. Grout works great because it is inexpensive and does not need sealer. Purchase grout in a color you like, and antique it with an exterior paint.

You may also use joint compound. Just be sure to cover the final project with a coat of clear waterproofing sealer. Occasionally, I will also use the Foam Finish.™ Treat this product the same as joint compound to seal it. I usually only use the Foam Finish™ method when the item will be partially covered by an awning or other structure.

Purchase joint compound in a ready-mixed form for convenience. It is very economical!

Water-Submersible Projects

You can create pond decorations and working fountains with foam! The main thing to remember is to *seal any seams* that will be under water. Use a water submersible product. I like to use Liquid Nails® for heavy duty construction to both join pieces and seal the seams. After that, I have two favorite methods you may choose from to cover the foam. First, you may use

Foam Finish™ is self-leveling to create a smooth surface.

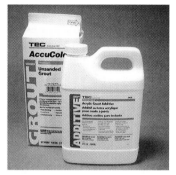

Tile grout is excellent for outdoor projects. Be sure to use an additive to make it weatherproof. It may be used in water-submersible projects.

tile grout and an additive to make it weather resistant. The grout may be tinted with acrylic paint or purchased pre-colored. You may also choose to paint it with an exterior paint after the grout has hardened. The only downfall of grout is that it is heavy.

The other method is to apply joint compound just like the indoor projects, and then seal it with one coat of basement water barrier paint. Finish off the project with an exterior paint and/or clear sealer.

While grout and joint compound are my favorite products to use for water-submersible projects, you may also use pre-mixed stucco, Durham's Rock Hard Water Putty™, quick plug (basement leak plug), and cement.

Covering Foam with Joint Compound

Drywall joint compound is a material typically used by contractors to finish walls in new construction. It is often referred to as "mud." The price and versatility of this material make it a terrific choice for many foam décor applications. Apply it with any combination of the applicators previously pictured. The forgiving properties of joint compound allow it to be textured or sanded perfectly smooth. You may choose to sand it while it is wet or dry.

Here are a few examples of items that may be used to create textures in joint compound.

To cover foam décor creations with joint compound, choose the combination of applicators that work best for the project. Apply the compound just thick enough to cover the holes of the foam. If a thick layer is applied and allowed to dry, it will crack more than a thinner (skim coat) layer that just covers the holes. Cracking is not necessarily bad for most of the foam décor projects in this book, but you should know this could happen. Use plastic putty knives to apply the compound to large areas.

Pallet knives (or craft sticks) are excellent for covering the ½" thick sides of the scrollwork projects in the book. Simply scrape joint compound onto the sides (as if icing a cake) with a pallet knife (or craft stick) then use your preferred sanding method to smooth. For relief-carved projects and boxes, paintbrushes are excellent for getting into tight spots and corners. After the project is completely covered where needed, sand the project (if a smooth finish is called for) with either the wet or dry method.

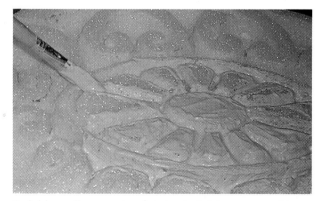

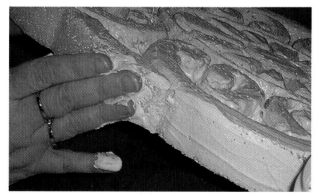

1. Add small amounts of water to joint compound in a bowl and stir until it reaches a velvety texture. Apply joint compound to the entire project, working from the deeper areas to the top. Cover the sides last. Apply just enough compound to cover the holes of the foam. For relief carved projects like this one, use a paintbrush (and your hands) to apply the compound.

2. It is helpful to use your hands to apply the compound to large areas such as the sides. You may use the joint compound straight from the bucket or add water as before. Use the way that works best for you.

Covering Foam with Foam Finish™

Foam Finish™ is a unique product that was created just for foam. It is used whenever you want a smooth finish on small to medium size projects. For best results, put down a layer of wax paper or foil on the work surface. Then, place scrap pieces of foam underneath the project. Next, simply stir the Foam Finish™ thoroughly until it has liquefied to a pancake batter consistency. Pour a generous coat on the project and spread with any of the same applicators used for the joint compound. Foam Finish™ is self leveling, so excess will run off onto the wax paper or foil. Allow the project to dry approximately 24 hours. You may speed up drying by placing the project in front of a fan or outside in the sun. After the project is dry, check to see if all the holes are covered. Generally, foam projects will require two coats of Foam Finish™.

1. Spread wax paper or foil over your work area. Elevate the project on a scrap of foam or plate. For balls, insert a skewer and place that in a scrap of foam. Stir Foam Finish™ until it is a pancake batter consistency; pour over the project.

2. Spread the Foam Finish™ over the project with a paintbrush or craft stick until it is covered. Apply more Foam Finish™ as needed.

3. Allow the covered project to dry several hours. Add another coat of Foam Finish™ if the texture of the foam holes is still apparent. Sand away any drips that may occur when the final coat is dry.

Covering Foam with Grout

Grout is an excellent material for outdoor projects and fountains. It is important to remember to use an additive to make the grout weather resistant. Be sure to work quickly! Pay attention to how smoothly you apply grout, because it will be nearly impossible to sand after it dries. You may add tint or acrylic paint to the grout while mixing, or use a pre-colored grout. Add a clear sealer to projects where the grout will be used without painting.

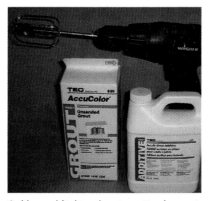

1. Use a kitchen beater attachment on a cordless drill to help stir grout. Do not use the kitchen mixer. The motor may burn up. Do not use the beater for food anymore.

2. Mix the proper amount of acrylic additive with grout. Allow the mixture to sit (slake) for about 10 minutes to work out bubbles. For foam décor projects, you will want to use the acrylic additive in place of water.

3. Apply the grout mixture to the foam project. Be aware of how you apply the grout. The pattern you apply will be the final result. If you are using the colored grout for your final project color, apply a clear brush-on water sealer after the grout has cured.

Tools and Materials

SANDING FOAM

Many projects need some smoothing after they have been covered with joint compound, Foam Finish™, or plaster. Following are wet and dry sanding techniques for the various covering materials.

Wet Sanding

In *Foam Décor*, wet sanding refers to smoothing joint compound with water while it is still wet. To wet sand, sprinkle or spray a little water on the project. Dip your fingers in water and apply gentle pressure to smooth the project to the desired texture. You may also wet a sponge with water and wipe the moistened project to smooth out large bumps. Use a paintbrush dipped in water to smooth tight areas and corners. If you remove too much compound at any point, simply reapply more joint compound. This method is great because it produces no dust.

1. A project that has been covered in joint compound may be smoothed (wet sanded) while it is still damp. After the project has been covered, allow it to sit for about an hour to set up, then proceed.

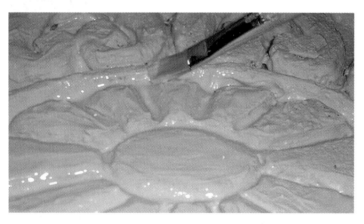

2. Use a paintbrush dipped in water to smooth the joint compound. You may also use your hands dipped in water. A wet sponge is helpful for smoothing large, lumpy areas. The sponge will take away the excess material.

3. Allow the smoothed project to dry for several hours. If there are still rough areas after the project has completely dried, use any of the dry sanding tools to smooth the joint compound.

Dry Sanding

Dry sanding refers to using traditional sanding methods and tools to smooth a foam décor project after the covering material has dried. This method may be done on foam that has been covered with joint compound, Foam Finish™, or plaster. Use metal files, emery boards, sandpaper, and/or a sanding sponge to sand off excess material until the desired texture is achieved. Always wear a dust mask when sanding these materials. They will generate a lot of dust. Wipe the project with cheesecloth or tack cloth after dry sanding to prepare it for painting. If you happen to sand all the way back to the foam holes, apply more of the covering material to the area.

An assortment of metal files help get into tight spots. The metal files are great because they do not clog up. If you use nail files, you will need to change them often.

1. Start by sanding the larger areas with either a sanding sponge (pictured) or sandpaper.

2. Use emery boards or metal files to define tight areas. It is helpful to elevate the project on scrap foam.

Additional Tools and Techniques

■ FLATTENING TOOLS

Occasionally, you will need to make the foam bend. This is impossible without treating the foam. You will use either a hammer, or for very thin foam, a pasta machine. If a pasta machine is used, you may not use it for food again. Choose inexpensive lightweight hammers to reduce strain on your wrist. You may use any of the types shown to get different effects. The large rubber mallet will cover more area. The ball peen is great for creating hammered metal looks. A rolling pin will not work. It will not flatten the foam properly.

To use the pasta machine:

1. A pasta machine is ideal for flattening foam.

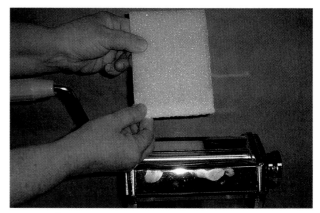

2. Cut a ½″ thick piece of foam with a serrated knife on all four sides. Do not use any factory edges. Pinch the foam on one end to help start it through the machine.

3. Secure the pasta machine to a worktable that is waist high for cranking. Set the machine to the thickest setting. Place the pinched end of the foam on the rollers. Begin cranking. Apply gentle pressure to the foam to help feed the foam through.

4. The flat foam is ready to be cut. The foam may crack a little in some places. This should not be a problem if you plan to use any of the foam covering techniques from this book. Place a pattern on the foam and trace it with a permanent marker. Cut the foam with scissors.

Measuring Tools

Clear acrylic rulers are wonderful measuring tools for working with foam. They have several grid marks that help you to achieve straight lines.

Working with Patterns

You may create your own patterns as I have for this book, or you may choose to use stencils. If you are creating your own patterns, try the Fiskars® Shape Cutter™. This tool has a blade that pivots, making tight cuts a breeze. Not only does it save time, but it is also ergonomic. Use short pins or tacks found in office stores to hold patterns to thin ½" thick foam. Straight pins work for thicker foam.

Some traditional tools for pattern cutting include a razor knife and scissors. These Softouch™ scissors have a spring mechanism and soft grip that make them easier to use than traditional scissors.

Stencils may be used as patterns for foam décor projects. Silhouette stencils are easiest to use. These stencils are different because you would normally paint the background versus the pattern.

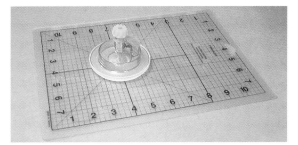

The Fiskars® Shape Cutter™ is an excellent time-saving alternative to a matte knife for cutting out patterns. To cut freehand patterns with this tool, place the pattern on the self-healing cutting mat. Adjust the blade so that the cutter sits flat on the work surface. While applying gentle pressure, guide the cutter along the pattern.

Connecting Foam Pieces

Foam décor projects are held together with either Beacon Hold the Foam!™ glue or Liquid Nails® for Heavy Duty Construction. The foam glue is great for most projects. When extra tough strength is required, you will use the Liquid Nails®. Note the type of Liquid Nails®. Although the company makes a formula for foam board, I have found that it takes too long to dry. The Heavy Duty type will create a quick permanent bond.

Greening pins are stronger than straight pins and are used in larger projects to reinforce layers and joined pieces. You can find these in the floral section of craft stores.

Flat-head pins are excellent for holding patterns to 1" or thicker foam and for reinforcing joined pieces.

Toothpicks may be used to join pieces as well. Be sure to choose thicker quality types, as the slivers will not hold up at all.

How to Create a Hanger

Many of the projects throughout the book require a hanger. Here is a simple hanger that will work for all of your needs. If you can find them, straw wreath hangers also work.

1. Use a 6" long piece of 18-gauge wire. Bend the wire in half like a hairpin (see photo).

2. Bend each prong in half in the same direction (see photo) and you are finished!

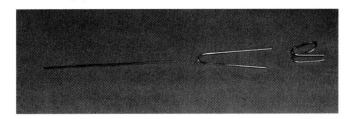

3. Insert the prongs of the hanger into the foam, and glue at each insertion point. A loop will be left on the outside of the foam to hang the project.

CHAPTER 2

Architectural Elegance

Time worn relics of *Foam Décor ...*

The projects in this chapter will add a feel of aged elegance to modern functionality in any room. Change the architecture of a room with a new arched doorway, or create a lovely planter for that troubled spot you have been waiting to fill. Turn to any page, and you will simply have to read on! Feel free to customize the colors to fit your own decor. If you enjoy the verdigris green patina, then go for it. There are no boundaries!

Gothic Floral Plaque

Create a piece of history. Influenced by Gothic friezes, this plaque is simple to make.

Level 1

Safety First!

• **When flattening the foam, wear eye protection. Pieces could fly!**

1. Attach the knife blade tip to the multi-tipped tool, and plug it in.

2. From the pattern sheet, cut out the pattern shapes with scissors.

3. Use the heated tool (see page 10 for tips) to cut the following items from the ½" thick sheet of foam: one 8" x 8" square, four leaves (Pattern A), five large petals (Pattern B), five small petals (Pattern C), two 1" x 1" squares.

4. Bevel (soften) the edges. Use the hammer to tap down the sharp edges of one side. Next, flip the piece over and tap these edges. Repeat this step for all pieces from step 3.

5. Flatten all of the cut pieces with a rubber mallet or hammer. Each piece will be a little more than ¼" thick.

6. Find the center of the 8" x 8" square. Using the pencil, score a diagonal line from one corner to the other. Repeat for the other two corners. Glue the 1" x 1" pieces in the center on top of each other.

7. Apply glue to the back of each leaf. Position the leaves along the scored diagonal lines. The longer tip on each leaf should fit in the corner of the plaque. Pin in place to secure.

8. Apply glue to the back of the larger petals. Position them around the center. The top edge of each petal should slightly overlap the shorter tips on each leaf. Pin in place to secure.

9. Apply glue to the back of the smaller petals. Position them around the center. The flat edge of each petal should touch or come close to the 1" square in the center. Pin in place to secure.

10. Cut the 1" balls in half. Roll each ball between your palms to soften the edges.

11. Create the center of the flower. To assemble the pieces in this step, apply glue to the backside of each whole ball. Insert a straight pin to secure. Glue a circle of half balls around the outer edge of the center area. The half balls should be pushed into each other to make a circle. Pack the center with more half balls. Build up the center with additional balls as needed to create a tightly packed cluster of balls.

12. Cover the surface with Foam Finish or drywall joint compound. Alternate between the paintbrushes to spread the finish. The goal is to make the plaque look as if it came from one large piece of material. Allow to dry overnight, or until hardened.

13. Apply a coat of the Shenandoah Taupe paint and allow to dry.

14. Antique the surface of the plaque with diluted paint. Mix one part Hot Springs Stones paint to one part water. Apply the paint with a paintbrush. Immediately blot away excess paint with a paper towel.

15. Create the hanger (see page 19). Insert the hanger wires up into the back of the plaque. Apply glue to the insertion to secure. Allow the glue to dry before hanging the plaque.

Materials

• 1 craft foam sheet, ½" x 12" x 36"
• 16 craft foam balls, 1" diameter
• Foam glue*
• Foam Finish* or ready-mix joint compound
• 1 qt. taupe paint, flat sheen*
• 1 qt. stone paint, flat sheen*
• 1" bristle paintbrush
• #12 flat paintbrush
• 6" of 18-gauge wire
• Flathead straight pins
• Disposable bowl
• Hot multi-tipped tool* and knife blade tip
• Rubber mallet (optional)
• Acrylic ruler*, hammer, paper towels, pencil, scissors*, wire cutters
* Used in this project: Beacon Hold the Foam!™ glue and Foam Finish™; Fiskars® Softouch™ scissors and acrylic ruler; Walnut Hollow Creative Versa-tool™, and Benjamin Moore Shenandoah Taupe and Hot Springs Stones paints.

Variations

• Try a circular medallion. All of the assembly steps apply; just use a disc as the base.

Medieval Ornamental Plaque

During the fifteenth century, much of the ornamentation consisted of geometric-shaped flowers and leaves. This project is an example of ornamentation from Lavenham Church, Suffolk.

Level 1

Safety First!

• **When flattening the foam, wear eye protection. Pieces could fly!**

1. From the pattern sheet, cut out the pattern shape with scissors.

2. Use the serrated knife to cut eight leaves (Pattern A) from the ½" thick foam. Cut one 8" x 8" piece from the ½" thick sheet of foam.

3. Bevel the edges of the square piece of foam. Shape the rough sides with your fingers or tap them with a mallet.

4. Flatten the leaves. Run each leaf through the pasta machine on the thickest setting. Trim the rough edges with scissors. If you do not have a pasta machine, use a rubber mallet to flatten the pieces.

5. Find the center of the 8" x 8" square. Using the pencil, score a diagonal line from one corner to the other. Repeat for the other two corners.

6. Cut the ball in half. Use the pencil to score lines into the ball. See Fig. 1 for line placement and pattern. Carve the lines to approximately ¾" depth with the same pencil.

7. Cut each egg in half with the serrated knife. Use the pencil to score and carve lines into the eggs. See Fig. 2 for line placement and pattern.

8. Apply glue to the back of a leaf. Position the leaves along the scored diagonal lines. The longer tip on each leaf should fit in the corner of the plaque. Pin in place to secure. Repeat for the other three corners.

9. Apply glue to the topside of one of the leaves from Step 8 around the edges. Place another leaf on top of this one. Pin around all edges except the end where the egg will be (refer to Fig. 2). Repeat for the other three corners.

Materials

- 1 craft foam sheet, ½" x 12" x 36"
- 2 craft foam hen eggs
- 2" craft foam ball
- Foam glue*
- Foam Finish™* or ready-mix joint compound
- 1 qt. taupe paint, flat sheen*
- 1 qt. stone paint, flat sheen*
- 1" bristle brush
- #12 flat paintbrush
- 6" of 18-gauge wire
- Flathead straight pins
- Disposable bowl
- Serrated knife
- Pasta machine (optional)
- Paper towels
- Acrylic ruler*, pencil, permanent marker, rubber mallet or hammer, scissors*, wire cutters
- * Used in this project: Beacon Hold the Foam!™ glue and Foam Finish™; Fiskars® Softouch™ scissors and acrylic ruler; and Benjamin Moore Shenandoah Taupe and Hot Springs Stones paints.

10. Apply glue to the back of an egg half. Position the piece just inside of the pocket created in Step 7. If the foam cracks slightly, do not worry. This will be disguised later. Repeat this step for the other three egg halves.

11. Cover the surface with Foam Finish™ or drywall joint compound. Alternate between the paintbrushes to spread the finish. Be sure to apply enough to fill in the areas where layers of petals meet. The goal is to make the plaque look as if it came from one large piece of material. Allow it to dry overnight, or until hardened. If necessary, wet sand the piece and/or apply another coat of Foam Finish™.

12. Apply a coat of the Shenandoah Taupe paint. Allow the paint to dry.

13. Antique the surface of the plaque with a mixture of one part Hot Springs Stones paint to one part water. Apply the paint with a sea sponge. Immediately blot away excess paint with a paper towel.

14. Create the hanger (see page 19). Insert the hanger wires up into the back of the plaque. Apply glue to the insertion to secure. Allow the glue to dry before hanging the plaque.

Variations

• The finished piece may be hung either as a square or in a diamond orientation.

Fig. 1

Fig. 2

Gothic Face Oil Lamp

The original face was found on wooden ornaments. I have added oil lamps to give this architectural fragment a purpose. The motif on the shelf is reminiscent of early English ornamentation found at Wells Cathedral.

Level 1

Safety First!

• **Wear eye protection while working with the rotary tool.**

   1. From the pattern sheet, cut out the pattern shape with scissors.

   2. Using a jigsaw (or coping saw), cut two 8" x 8" squares from the foam block. Pin the pattern to one of the squares. Using the rotary tool (see page 12), carve the pattern into the square. Use Fig. 3 as a reference after the pattern is torn up.

   3. Glue the carved piece to the other square. Allow the pieces to dry for about 45 minutes.

   4. Use both ends of the ball peen hammer to distress the straight edges of the un-carved block. Distress the sides of the now 4" thick square in the same manner to make it look like a chunk of stone. Distressing makes a new item look worn or weathered. The more "beat up" the square looks, the more distressed it is.

   5. Carve three holes into the top of the carving. Mark three spots, spacing them evenly apart. Place an oil lamp on the spots and trace around it with the pencil. Use the rotary tool to carve the holes. Start by going around the circle, and remove the excess. Next, carve deeper and into the bottom of the hole. Repeat this process until the oil lamp fits easily in and out of the hole. The final depth of the hole depends upon how tall your oil lamp insert is. The wick should be about ¾" above the foam when the candle is in place. Remove the oil lamps, and set them aside.

Materials

- 1 craft foam block, 2" x 12" x 18"
- Foam glue*
- Joint compound
- Acrylic paint, Olive Green Dark*
- Faux Stone spray paint, Charcoal Sand*
- Glazing medium*
- #12 round paintbrush
- 3 round votive-shaped oil lamps, 2" x 2"
- Flathead straight pins
- Disposable bowl
- Rotary tool*
- Jigsaw or coping saw
- Ball peen hammer
- Acrylic ruler*, paper towels, pencil, scissors*

* Used in this project: Krylon Make It Stone® paint; Beacon Hold the Foam!™ glue; Fiskars® Softouch™ scissors and acrylic ruler; Plaid Enterprises Folk Art® acrylic paint and glazing medium; and Dremel Multi-Pro rotary tool.

6. Apply joint compound with your hand to fill in the crack between the glued pieces. Allow the joint compound to dry.

7. Apply several coats of the faux stone paint until the entire project is covered and the holes in the foam are not visible. Follow the manufacturer's instructions for using the paint. Allow the project to dry overnight.

8. Antique the surface of the plaque with a mixture of diluted paint. Mix one part Olive Green paint to one part glazing medium. Apply the glaze with a paintbrush. Immediately blot away excess paint with a paper towel. The lower carved areas should have more paint in them. This will give the effect of moss growing in the cracks. Be sure to keep the carving laying flat while the paint dries, or some of the paint may run.

9. After the project dries, place the glass oil lamps in the holes and enjoy your art!

Variations

• You may use a potato peeler as a carving tool for this project. However, the rotary tool is faster and gives the best results.

Fig. 3

Medieval Carved Shelf

This fabulous foam shelf is a great way to display your other foam creations.

Level 1

Safety First!
• **Wear eye protection while working with the rotary tool.**

1. From the pattern sheet, cut out the pattern shape with scissors.

2. Using a jigsaw (or coping saw), cut the following items from the 1½" thick sheet of foam: one 6" x 34½" rectangle, one 4" x 28½" rectangle.

3. Pin the pattern to the 2" thick foam sheet. Cut out the shape with the jigsaw (or coping saw).

4. Use the rotary tool to carve the pattern into the 2" thick foam shape. Carve the large, black area to about ¾" depth. Carve the smaller, thin lines to about ¼" depth. See page 12 for more information on how to use the rotary tool. Use Fig. 4 as a reference once the pattern is torn up.

5. Distress the edges of the square pieces. Shape rough sides by tapping them with the hammer. Be sure to round all corners.

6. Assemble the parts. Glue the smaller rectangle to the larger one. Center and line up the small rectangle so that one of its longer edges is even with the long edge of the larger piece. These should rest flat on the wall. Add the carved piece to the bottom center of the small rectangle. The back should be even with the other two layers. All three layers will rest flat on the wall when hung.

Materials
- Craft foam sheet, 1½" x 12" x 36"
- Craft foam sheet, 2" x 12" x 36"
- Joint compound
- 1 qt. taupe paint, flat sheen*
- 1 qt stone paint, flat sheen*
- 1" bristle brush
- #12 flat paintbrush
- 18" of 18-gauge wire, cut into 3 equal pieces
- Flathead pins
- Floral greening pins
- Disposable bowl
- Jigsaw or coping saw
- Rotary tool*
- 2" putty knife
- Heavy duty glue*
- Caulking gun
- Paper towels
- Acrylic ruler*, hammer, scissors*, wire cutters
- * Used in this project: Fiskars® Softouch™ scissors and acrylic ruler; Liquid Nails® for Heavy-Duty Construction glue; Dremel Multi-Pro rotary tool, and Benjamin Moore Shenandoah Taupe and Hot Springs Stones paints.

7. Reinforce the layers. Use greening pins to help hold the layers of foam together. Insert several of these pins through the top rectangle to connect it to the smaller layer. Flip the shelf so the top flat layer is resting on the work surface. Insert one prong of the pin into one layer, and insert the other prong into the other one. Do this in several places between the large and small rectangles, and then between the small rectangle and the carved piece. Allow the glue to dry before you continue.

8. Cover the project with drywall joint compound. Alternate between your hands, a putty knife, and a paintbrush. Use what feels comfortable to you. Be sure to apply enough to fill in the areas where layers of foam meet. You will want to make the shelf look as if it came from one large piece of material. See chapter one for more information on how to apply joint compound. Allow your piece to dry for about two hours.

9. Wet sand the piece until the rough peaks are softened. Apply another coat of joint compound if necessary. Some cracking occurs as the piece dries if you apply a thick coat of joint compound. This is not a problem if you do not mind the ancient look. If you want to get rid of the cracks, fill in with more joint compound.

10. Apply a coat of the Shenandoah Taupe paint. Allow the paint to dry.

11. Antique the surface of the plaque with a mixture of one part Hot Springs Stones paint to one part water. Apply the thinned paint with a paintbrush. Immediately blot away excess pant with a paper towel.

12. Create three hangers (see page 19). Position the hangers evenly across the back on the middle "layer" of foam. Insert the hanger wires up into the back of the shelf. Apply glue to the insertions to secure. Allow the glue to dry before hanging the shelf.

Variations

• This shelf will hold 10 to 20 lbs. (more or less depending on how thick you have applied the joint compound). To keep the shelf from denting, you may wish to cover the top shelf with a layer of tile grout. See Tools and Techniques for how to use grout.

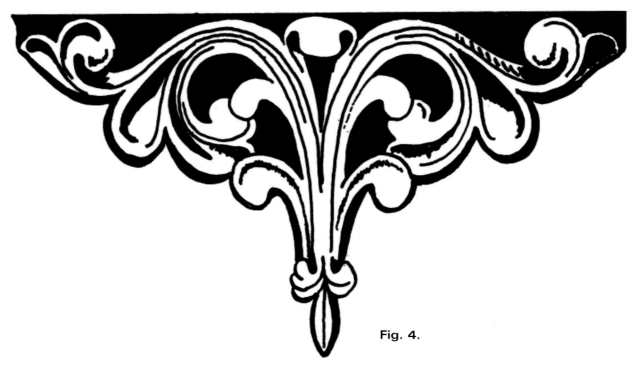

Fig. 4.

French Scroll Sconce

A French ironwork banister inspired this versatile sconce. It is perfect for holding a scarf or small items. The scroll finial keeps fabric from sliding off the front.

Level 1

Safety First!

• **Wear eye protection while working with the rotary tool.**

1. Use the shape cutter to cut the pattern from the pattern sheet. Be sure to cut out all of the black areas on the inside of the pattern.

2. Pin the pattern to the foam block. Use the coping saw (or jigsaw) to cut around the outside of the pattern.

3. Carve the open areas on the inside of the pattern with the rotary tool (or potato peeler) to about ¾" depth. Remove the pattern. Use Fig. 5 as a reference while carving.

4. Flip the carved piece over to the un-carved side. Flip the pattern over and pin it on. Carve this side.

5. Repeat Steps 2 to 5 to make the other sconce.

6. Cut the dowel into two 2" long pieces. Set one piece aside. Dip one end of the other piece into glue, and insert it into the top of one sconce. Position the dowel about 2" from the back. Repeat for the second sconce.

7. Cover the surface of each sconce with Foam Finish™ or joint compound. See chapter one for more information on how to use Foam Finish™. If using Foam Finish™, allow the project to dry until hardened. If using joint compound, wet sand the project after two hours.

8. Start the Scroll Finial(s) while the sconces are drying. See page 30.

9. After the sconces have completely hardened, dry sand if necessary.

Materials

- Craft foam block, 2" x 12" x 18"
- Foam Finish™* or joint compound
- 1 qt. taupe paint, flat sheen*
- 1 qt stone paint, flat sheen*
- #12 flat paintbrush
- 12" of 18-gauge wire, cut into two equal pieces
- Flathead straight pins
- ⅛" dowel, 4" long
- Rotary tool* or potato peeler
- Shape cutter*
- Cutting mat*
- Coping saw (jigsaw)
- Pallet knife
- Glue*, pencil, scissors*
- * Used in this project: Fiskars® Shape Cutter™, cutting mat, and Softouch™ scissors; Beacon Foam Finish™ and Hold the Foam!™ glue; Dremel Multi-Pro rotary tool, and Benjamin Moore Shenandoah Taupe and Hot Springs Stones paints.

Foam Décor

30

10. Apply a coat of the Shenandoah Taupe paint. Allow the paint to dry.

11. Antique the surface of the plaque with a mixture of one part Hot Springs Stones paint to one part water. Apply the thinned paint with a paintbrush. Immediately blot away excess paint with a paper towel. Allow the project to dry completely before hanging, or some dripping may occur. To help speed the drying, use a hair dryer on the lowest setting.

12. Make a hanger for each sconce (see page 19). Center the hanger on each sconce. Insert the hanger wires up into the back. Apply glue to the insertions to secure. Allow the glue to dry before hanging.

Fig. 5

Variations

- Add a hole through the side of each sconce for a more traditional scarf holder. Slice a rough hole with a serrated knife (about 2" diameter). Clean up the roughness with a round file or the rotary tool. Continue with the covering and painting steps.
- You may create one 4" wide sconce. Simply cut two sconce shapes from the block and glue them together. Carve each side as in Steps 4 and 5. Continue with Steps 7 to 11. Create two hangers to support the shelf.
- Adapt the pattern to make interesting embellishments. The Accent Molding project pictured at the end of this chapter in the gallery incorporates this scroll. I used ½" thick foam in this case to make the scroll fit seamlessly with the moldings (which are also carved from craft foam).
- If you do not want to use a finial, do not insert the craft stick in step 6.

Scroll Finial

Level 1

This elegant finial completes the French Scroll Sconce and keeps your fabric from falling.

Safety First!

- **Use goggles and a fume mask when working with the heated knife.**
- **Be sure to sit the tool on a proper stand. It gets very hot!**
- **Use pliers to tighten the tip if it becomes loose.**

1. Attach the knife blade into the multi-tipped tool and plug it in.

2. Use the shape cutter to cut the finial pattern from the pattern sheet.

3. Pin the pattern to the foam. Cut around the pattern with the heated knife blade.

4. Repeat Step 3 for the other finial.

5. Unplug the heated tool. Once the tool is cool, remove the knife tip. Replace it with a straight tip, and plug the tool back in. Melt a hole through each finial, large enough to fit your marble snugly. Remove the marble and set aside.

6. Cover the surface of each finial with Foam Finish™ or joint compound. If using Foam Finish™, allow the finials to dry until hardened. If using joint compound, wet sand the finials now, and then allow them to dry.

7. After the sconces have completely hardened, dry sand if necessary.

8. Apply a coat of clear sealer and allow it to dry.

9. Apply enough Instant Iron paint to cover the entire finial. You may have to apply a second coat after the first has dried to the touch. Allow the finials to dry for 12 hours.

10. Apply a coat of Instant Rust. Allow the paint to react for a few hours. Apply another coat if desired. Wait 24 hours before adding any more coats. As you add more coats, the color will become more brown and red.

11. Insert the marbles. They should not push all the way through. If the hole is very large, use some clear glue to secure them.

12. Attach the finials to the French Scroll Sconces. Gently slide the finials onto the wooden dowels to secure.

Materials

- Craft foam sheet, ½" x 12" x 36"
- Shape cutter*
- Cutting mat*
- Foam Finish™* or joint compound
- Instant Iron paint*
- Instant Rust paint*
- Clear sealer*
- 1" bristle paintbrush
- #12 round paintbrush
- 2 marbles, ½" diameter
- Flathead pins
- Hot multi-tipped tool*
- 10mm ball tip pins
- * Used in this project: Beacon Foam Finish™; Fiskars® Shape Cutter™ and cutting mat; Walnut Hollow Creative Versa-tool™; and Modern Options Sophisticated Finishes paints and sealer.

Variations

- Try using other foam shapes, (such as eggs) as finials.
- Check out the sun finial in Chapter 3 for another idea.

German Scrollwork Cornice

Hidden motifs and graceful curves accent this realistic foam décor cornice. Only you will know it is made from foam.

Level 1

Materials
• Craft foam sheet, ½" x 12" x 36"
• Joint compound
• Clear sealer
• Instant Iron paint*
• Instant Rust paint*
• 1" bristle paintbrush
• #12 flat paintbrush
• 10mm ball tip pins
• Shape cutter*
• Cutting mat*
• Pallet knife
• Disposable bowl
• Hot multi-tipped tool* with knife blade and straight tips
* Used in this project: Fiskars® Shape Cutter™ and cutting mat; Walnut Hollow Creative Versa-tool™ heated creative tool; and Modern Options Sophisticated Finishes paints and sealer.

Safety First!
• **Use goggles and a fume mask when working with the heated knife.**
• **Be sure to sit the tool on a proper stand. It gets very hot!**
• **Use pliers to tighten the tip if it becomes loose.**

1. Attach the knife blade tip to the multi-tipped tool, and plug it in.

2. Use the shape cutter to cut the pattern from the pattern sheet. Cut out all of the black areas of the pattern.

3. Pin the pattern to the foam with ball tip pins. Be sure to pin down all scroll pieces that may pop up. Use the hot knife to cut out all of the areas inside the pattern first, then cut around the pattern perimeter. Leaving the excess on the outside will help keep the foam stable. Do not try to cut out the tiny round holes yet.

4. Unplug the heated tool. Once the tool is cool, remove the knife tip. Replace with the straight blunt tip and plug the tool back in. Melt a hole through the areas where the tiny holes are.

5. Cover the cornice with joint compound. Alternate between the pallet knife and a paintbrush. Be sure to apply enough to cover the holes of the foam. Allow the project to dry until hardened.

6. Wet sand the cornice. Apply another coat of joint compound if holes are really obvious. The Iron paint will help fill in some shallow holes. Allow the cornice to dry once more if another coat is applied.

7. Apply a coat of clear sealer to the cornice and allow it to dry.

8. Apply enough Instant Iron paint to cover any parts that will show in the final piece. You may add a second coat, once the paint is dry to the touch. Allow the project to dry for 12 hours.

9. Apply a coat of Instant Rust. Allow the paint to react for a few hours. Apply another coat if desired. Wait 24 hours before adding any more coats. The more coats that are added, the more brown and red a piece with typically get.

10. Hang your masterpiece and enjoy it every day. I still do!

Variations
• The finished piece is 12" x 36". If your window is six feet wide, try making two cornices and hang them right next to each other. It makes a truly dramatic effect!
• Create an amazing scrollwork wall piece! This piece would look great on a wall grouped with objects or alone. For that extra flair, make two and hang them one over the other, flipped so they are mirroring each other. This will make a 24" x 36" oval shape. What fun!

French Ironwork Planter

A graceful scrolling openwork design adorns this unique planter. Line the inside with moss to soften the look of the faux ironwork.

Level 2

Safety First!

- **Use goggles and a fume mask when working with the heated knife.**
- **Be sure to sit the tool on a proper stand. It gets very hot!**
- **Use pliers to tighten the tip if it becomes loose.**

1. Attach the knife blade tip to the multi-tipped tool, and plug it in.

2. Flatten the wide end of each egg by pushing it on your work surface.

3. Apply glue to a toothpick and insert it into the large end of one egg. Leave about 1" of the toothpick sticking out of the foam egg. Repeat this step for the other five eggs.

4. Apply joint compound to each egg with your hands. Insert the toothpick into the scrap piece of foam to dry. Wet sand each egg. Set aside for later.

5. Use the shape cutter to cut the patterns from the pattern sheet. Cut out all of the black areas inside of each pattern.

6. Measure to 18" on the foam sheet, and mark a line with the permanent marker. Use the heated tool to cut the line. Set the smaller piece aside.

7. Pin the longer pattern to the larger piece of foam with ball tip pins. Line up two of the sides of the pattern with factory edges of the foam. Line up the ruler with the other long side of the pattern that does not have the factory edge. Using the heated knife blade, score the blade along the edge of the ruler. Remove the ruler, and carefully break the foam sheet.

8. Use the heated blade to cut out all of the open areas of the pattern.

9. Using the other 18" long foam piece and the same pattern piece, repeat Steps 7 and 8 to create another long side.

10. Cut out the bottom of the box. Measure a 5" x 18" piece from the foam piece you sat aside. Cut it with the heated blade.

11. Align the smaller pattern with one of the corners (factory edges) of the remaining foam piece and pin it. Cut out this pattern in the same manner as the previous steps. Repeat to create a second short (side) piece.

Materials

- Craft foam sheet, ½" x 12" x 36"
- 6 craft foam "hen" eggs
- Scrap piece of foam approx. 8" long
- Acrylic paint*: Linen, Asphaltum*
- Glazing medium*
- Joint compound*
- 1" bristle paintbrush
- #12 round paintbrush
- 4 floral foam bricks, 3"x 4"x 8"
- 3 artificial tulip bushes
- Reindeer moss
- Sheet moss
- Greening pins
- Permanent marker
- Disposable bowl
- 10mm ball tip pins
- Paper towels
- Toothpicks
- Shape cutter*
- Cutting mat*
- Hot multi-tipped tool and knife blade tip*
- Pallet knife
- Glue*

* Used in this project: Syndicate Sales Floralfoam®; Beacon Hold the Foam!™ glue; Fiskars® Shape Cutter™ and cutting mat; Walnut Hollow Creative Versatool™; and Plaid Enterprises Folk Art® paints and glazing medium.

Variations

• Change your flowers with the seasons for a fresh look!

12. Assemble the box. Apply glue to a long side of the 5" x 18" (bottom) piece. Attach one of the longer carved pieces. Cut toothpicks in half and insert them where the two pieces are joined.

13. Repeat Step 12 to assemble the other long side.

14. Add the short sides. Apply glue to all edges to be joined, and insert toothpicks to strengthen these areas. Let the glue dry for about 45 minutes before starting the next step.

15. Cover the box with joint compound. Alternate between the pallet knife and round paintbrush as applicators. You do not have to cover the inside of the box. Wet sand the compound after about two hours. Allow the box to dry several hours, until hardened

16. After the box has completely hardened, dry sand any rough, undefined areas. See Chapter 1 for information on dry sanding.

17. Glue the legs (eggs) to the planter. For each egg, add glue to the egg and then insert the toothpick into the bottom of the planter.

18. Apply a coat of Linen paint. Allow it to dry.

19. Antique the project with a mixture of diluted paint. Mix one part Asphaltum paint to one part glazing medium, and then apply the glaze with a paintbrush. Immediately blot away excess paint with a paper towel. Allow the pitted areas to absorb more of the paint than the smoother areas.

20. To achieve the look shown: Line the planter with green reindeer moss. Add the floral foam bricks to the inside. Lay two in the bottom, and add two more on top of those. Tuck more moss around the sides if needed. Insert the three artificial tulip bushes into the foam, spacing them evenly. Support the bottom of the planter with one hand while pressing the tulips in with the other to keep from breaking through the bottom of the planter. Add sheet moss to the top of the foam bricks where the tulips do not cover. Use greening pins to hold the sheet moss in place. Bend and adjust the blooms for a natural look.

Fanlight Votive

In this interesting twist on the votive candleholder, candlelight glows beautifully from behind the fanlight design.

Level 1

- **Use goggles and a fume mask when working with the heated knife.**
- **Be sure to sit the tool on a proper stand. It gets very hot!**
- **Use pliers to tighten the tip if it becomes loose.**

1. Attach the knife blade tip to the multi-tipped tool, and plug it in.

2. Use the shape cutter to cut the pattern from the pattern sheet.

3. Pin the pattern to the ½" thick foam with ball tip pins. Cut out the pattern with the heated knife blade.

4. Cut the 1" x 6" x 12" block of foam in half lengthwise with the heated tool to get two 1" x 3" x 12" pieces. Cut 3" off of one piece to get a 9" long piece.

5. Cut the wreath in half. Glue the carved piece in the center of the cut wreath. Apply glue to each tip that touches the wreath. Pin in place.

6. Glue the pieces from Step 5 to the edge of the 1" x 3" x 9" block. Use a greening pin on each side where the wreath meets the block to secure. Insert these pins from the bottom of the block. Use flathead pins to attach the center of the carved piece to the block.

7. Create a hole in the block behind the center of the carved area with the glass peg on the candleholder. Remove the rubber piece from the glass peg light. Insert the glass piece into the foam then remove it.

8. Cover the cracks where the wreath and block meet. Use spackling paste or joint compound to fill the cracks.

9. Cover each sconce with Foam Finish™ (or joint compound). See chapter one for more information on using Foam Finish™ or joint compound. Allow the project to dry until hardened.

10. Dry sand the project if necessary.

11. Apply a coat of Linen paint. Allow it to dry.

12. Antique the project. Mix one part Asphaltum paint to one part glazing medium then apply the glaze with a paintbrush. Immediately blot away excess paint with a paper towel. The lower carved areas should have more paint in them.

13. Insert the glass piece in the hole, and then add a votive candle.

Materials

- Craft foam sheet, ½" x 12" x 36"
- Craft foam block, 1" x 6" x 12"
- Round craft foam wreath, ½" thick x 1" face x 9"
- Foam Finish™* or joint compound
- Spackling paste or joint compound
- Glass votive peg light
- Acrylic paint*: Linen, Asphaltum
- Glazing medium*
- 1" bristle paintbrush
- #12 round paintbrush
- Flathead pins
- Greening pins
- Paper towels
- 10mm ball tip pins
- Hot multi-tipped tool and knife blade tip*
- Shape cutter*
- Cutting mat*
- Glue*

*Used in this project: Beacon Hold the Foam!™ glue and Foam Finish™; Fiskars® Shape Cutter™ and cutting mat; Walnut Hollow Creative Versatool™; and Plaid Enterprises Folk Art® paint and glazing medium.

Variations

- Enlarge the wreath size and center pattern to create a large fanlight wall piece. Add a rectangle on the bottom to get the finished shape. The width of this piece will depend on the diameter of your wreath.
- You will have enough materials to create two fanlight votives.

Filigree Accent Lamp

Level 2

Whimsical animal legs adorn this lamp that began as a plastic vase and pieces of foam. You will enjoy the warm flattering glow this lamp gives off.

Safety First!

- **Use goggles and a fume mask when working with the heated knife.**
- **Be sure to sit the tool on a proper stand. It gets very hot!**
- **Use pliers to tighten the tip if it becomes loose.**

1. Attach the knife blade tip to the multi-tipped tool, and plug it in.

2. Use the shape cutter to cut the pattern from the pattern sheet. Cut out all of the black areas of the pattern. Pin the pattern to the ½" thick foam.

3. Use the heated blade to cut out the leg pattern. To shape the foam areas where the knife does not reach easily, use the emory board. Repeat this step for three more legs.

4. Unplug the heated tool. Once the tool is cool, remove the knife tip. Replace it with the straight tip, and plug the tool back in.

5. Bevel the edges of the disc by rolling the edges on your worktable.

6. Melt a hole in the center of the vase large enough for the the threaded pipe (all thread), included with the socket kit, to fit through. Be sure to line up the vase on the disc. Mark a dot on the inside of the vase where the hole will be made. Turn the vase upside down, and insert the hot tip into the vase. Twist the tool to move the melting plastic around. Allow the tool to penetrate all the way down to the larger shaft that the straight bit screws into. Move the tool in a circular motion to enlarge the hole until the correct size is achieved.

7. Mark the center of the disc and melt a hole large enough for the all-thread to fit through.

8. Glue and pin the legs to the disc. Position the legs one across from the other. The straight piece that attaches to the disc should stop just short of the hole created in Step 7.

9. Cover the surface of the base with Foam Finish™ or joint compound. Wet sand if using joint compound. See chapter one for more information on sanding Foam Finish™ or joint compound. Allow the project to dry until hardened.

10. Start decorating the vase with handmade paper. Tear the sheets of paper into random pieces. Leave no finished edges. Put the paper in piles, or mix them up to grab at random. Working in small sections, apply a light coat of decoupage glue to the vase with the foam paintbrush. Randomly add pieces of torn paper, overlapping one anoth-

Materials

- Craft foam sheet, ½" x 12" x 36"
- Craft foam disc, 1" x 4"
- 10" tall Scallop clear plastic vase with a 4" diameter bottom*
- Foam Finish™* or joint compound
- Foam glue*
- Instant Iron paint*
- Instant Rust paint*
- Clear sealer*
- 1" bristle paintbrush
- #12 round paintbrush
- 1" foam paintbrush
- Emory board
- Lamp cord with plug
- Porcelain lamp socket kit
- Cord switch (optional)
- Flame shape iridescent light buib (25 watt or less)
- ¾ yd. beaded fringe, Celadon
- ¾ yd. upholstery trim, Celadon
- 4 sheets handmade paper, Chocolate, Sage, Tan, Ivory, 8½" x 11" each
- Flathead pins
- 10mm ball tip pins
- Decoupage glue*
- Shape cutter*
- Cutting mat*
- Hot multi-tipped tool* with knife blade tip
- Hot glue gun and sticks
- Permanent marker
- Tiny Phillips head screwdriver (to fit screws in the socket)
- Wire cutters
- * Used in this project: Syndicate Sales Plastifoam® plastic vase; Beacon Hold the Foam!™ glue and Foam Finish™; Fiskars® Shape Cutter™ and cutting mat; Plaid Enterprises Modge Podge®; Walnut Hollow Creative Versa-tool™; and Modern Options Sophisticated Finishes paints and sealer.

- Many vase shapes will work for this type of project. Have fun experimenting! If you want the exact vase shown, it can be found at most florist shops.
- Choose different color and texture combinations of handmade papers.
- Try cutting out the leaf shapes from the handmade paper with the Leaves Template for the Shape Cutter™. You will need extra paper since the leaves are irregularly shaped, but the layered effect is great! To help the shape cutter blade guide through the handmade paper without snagging, use a scrap piece of paper on top of the handmade paper. Place the template on top of the layers. Always keep a fresh blade in the cutter to prevent snags.

er. Add more decoupage glue to the top of the positioned pieces. Repeat this process for the entire vase.

11. Once the base has hardened, dry sand if necessary.

12. Apply a coat of clear sealer and allow it to dry.

13. Apply enough Instant Iron paint to cover the base. You may add a second coat after the first has dried to the touch. Allow the base to dry for 12 hours.

14. Apply a coat of Instant Rust. Allow the paint to react for a few hours. Apply another coat if desired. Wait 24 hours before adding any more coats. The more coats that are added, the more brown and red a piece will typically get.

15. By now, the vase should be decorated and dry. Hot glue the fringe to the top edge of the vase. Cover the unattractive banding of the fringe. Hot glue the upholstery trim over it.

16. Hot glue the vase to the base. Allow it to set up before proceeding.

17. Start assembling the lamp. Feed the hex nut (from the socket kit) onto the cord first. Next, add the long piece of all thread. Then, feed the lamp (base and vase) onto the cord.

18. Wire the cord onto the socket. While working with the cord and socket, pull the cord up through the vase. Sit the vase on the floor to help keep it out of the way. The back of the socket has easy-to-follow instructions, showing how to wire on the cord. The only thing that is not

clear is what the ribbed cord is referring too. Pick up the cord and feel each side. One is smooth and the other is rough. The rough one is the ribbed cord.

19. Screw the all thread into the end of the socket. Insert the all thread through the hole in the bottom of the vase. Once the all thread is attached to the socket, pull the excess wire through the bottom of the lamp. Turn the hex nut on the all thread to tighten the socket to the base.

20. Add the switch. Follow the easy instructions on the back of the package.

21. Add the bulb, and plug in your creation!

Oval Cartouche

The unconventional shape and interlocking scrolls make this design interesting and versatile. Use it to adorn a wall, shelf, or even as a medallion for a window treatment.

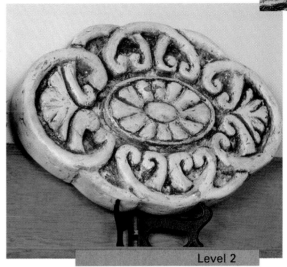

Level 2

Safety First!

• **Wear eye protection while working with the rotary tool.**

1. Cut the pattern shape from the pattern sheet with scissors.

2. Pin the pattern to the foam sheet. Cut out the shape with the saw.

3. Use the rotary tool to carve the pattern into the foam. See Chapter 1 for more information on how to use the rotary tool. The final depth of the carved areas should be about ¾". The thin lines should be about ¼" deep. Use Fig. 6 as a reference after the pattern is torn up.

4. Cover the project with joint compound, alternating between your hands, the pallet knife, and the paintbrush. Allow your piece to dry overnight or until hardened.

5. Wet sand the plaque until the rough peaks are softened. Apply another coat of joint compound if holes are still apparent. Some cracking occurs if you apply a thick coat of joint compound. This is not a problem, if you do not mind the ancient look. If you want to get rid of the cracks, fill in with more joint compound.

6. Apply a coat of the Linen paint. Allow the paint to dry.

7. Antique the plaque with the Antiquing Medium. Apply the medium with a paintbrush. Immediately wipe and blot away excess paint with a paper towel.

8. Create a hanger (see page 19). Position the hanger in the center of the backside of the oval. Insert the hanger wires up into the back of the shelf. Apply glue to the insertions to secure. Allow the glue to dry before hanging the finished piece.

Materials

• Craft foam sheet, 2" x 12" x 18"
• Joint compound
• Acrylic paint, Linen*
• Antiquing medium, Apple Butter Brown*
• 1" bristle brush
• Flathead pins
• 6" of 18-gauge wire
• Wire cutters
• Paper towels
• Jigsaw or coping saw
• Sanding sponge
• Pallet knife
• Rotary tool*
• Scissors*
• Disposable bowl

*Used in this project: Fiskars® Softouch™ scissors; Dremel Multi-Pro rotary tool; and Plaid Enterprises Folk Art® paint and antiquing medium.

Fig. 6

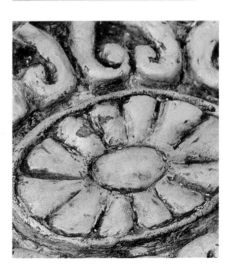

Victorian Silhouette

Layers of foam create depth, and a porcelain crackle finish adds a touch of age.

Safety First!

- **Use goggles and a fume mask when working with the heated knife.**
- **Be sure to sit the tool on a proper stand. It gets very hot!**

Level 1

1. Attach the knife blade tip to the multi-tipped tool, and plug it in.

2. Use scissors to cut out the silhouette pattern(s) that you wish to make from the pattern sheet. Choose from the mirror images.

3. Pin the pattern to the foam with the short pins. Cut around the pattern with the heated knife blade. Use Fig. 7 as a reference after the pattern is torn up.

4. Cut out the hair and scroll at the bottom of the pattern. Set aside the neck and face portion of the pattern.

5. Pin the hair and scroll onto the ½" thick foam sheet. Cut out the shapes with the heated blade.

6. Begin carving the details inside each pattern. Use the pencil to score the lines. Remove the pattern.

7. Carve the lines deeper. Use either the pencil to deepen all of the details or change the heat tool to the straight blunt tip. Be sure to unplug the blade and allow it to cool before touching the tool.

8. Place the neck and face pattern back on the first large piece. Carve the eye and nose details. Trace the eye and nose details with a pencil. Remove the pattern, and carve the lines deeper.

9. Glue the carved hair and scroll on top of the larger piece. Pin in place to secure. Insert the pins at an angle so they do not poke through the back.

10. Use spackling paste (or joint compound) to fill the crack where the layers meet.

11. Cover the silhouette with Foam Finish™ (or joint compound). Alternate between the pallet knife and a paintbrush. Be sure to apply enough to cover the holes of the foam. Allow the project to dry until hardened.

12. Dry sand the project after it hardens, if necessary.

13. Apply a coat of Linen paint. Allow to dry.

14. Using the Eggshell Crackle kit, apply a coat of Step 1. Allow this to dry.

15. Apply Step 2 in the Eggshell Crackle kit. Allow to dry.

16. Antique the project to bring out the cracks and carved details. Mix one part Burnt Umber paint with one part glazing medium, and then apply the glaze with a paintbrush. Immediately blot away excess paint with a paper towel. Use the paintbrush to get paint in tight areas. The lower carved areas should have more paint in them.

17. Create a hanger with the wire (see page 19). Insert the hanger wires up into the back of the plaque. Apply glue at the insertion to secure. Allow the glue to dry before hanging the project.

Materials

- Craft foam sheet, ½" x 12" x 36"
- Spackling paste or joint compound
- Foam Finish™* or joint compound
- Acrylic paint, Linen and Burnt Umber*
- Eggshell crackle medium kit*
- Glazing medium*
- 1" bristle paintbrush
- #12 round paintbrush
- Flathead pins
- 6" of 18-gauge wire
- 10mm ball tip pins
- Wire cutters
- Paper towel
- Hot multi-tipped tool* with knife blade and straight tips
- Pallet knife
- Glue*, pencil, scissors*

*Used in this project: Beacon Hold the Foam!™ glue and Foam Finish™; Fiskars® Softouch™ scissors; Walnut Hollow Creative Versa-tool™; and Plaid Enterprises Folk Art® paint, glazing medium, and Eggshell crackle kit.

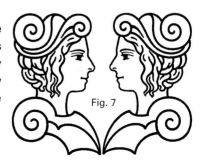

Fig. 7

Rusted Key and Keyplate

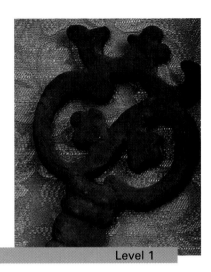

An over scale key and plate are beautifully displayed as collectible treasures in a regal shadow box.

Level 1

- **Use goggles and a fume mask when working with the heated knife.**
- **Be sure to sit the tool on a proper stand. It gets very hot!**

1. Attach the knife blade tip to the multi-tipped tool, and plug it in.

2. Use the shape cutter (or scissors) to cut the patterns from the pattern sheet. Be sure to cut out the black areas of the key top and key plate patterns.

3. Pin the patterns to the ½" thick foam. Cut out each pattern with the heated knife blade. See Chapter 1 for how to use the multi-tipped heat tool.

4. Use scissors to cut out the part of the key plate pattern that is on either side of the keyhole. Pin the pattern to a piece of ½" thick foam, and cut it out. Use the hammer to gently flatten this piece to about ¼" thickness. Glue it on the foam key plate (around the key-hole).

5. Unplug the heated tool. Once the tool is cool, remove the knife tip. Replace with the straight, blunt tip and plug the tool back in. Melt holes in the key plate where the black circles are on the pattern.

6. Crush four of the 1½" balls to about ¼" thickness. Start crushing by flattening each end of the ball on a hard surface. Next, place a sturdy item such as a small book on top of the ball and push to the desired thickness.

7. Crush the last ball just until flat on each end. Leave it thicker and more rounded than the other balls.

8. Cut a rectangle from the 1" block that measures 1" x 7". Use a scrap piece of foam to begin sanding away the corners of the rectangle. Next, place the sanding sponge in one hand and grip the rectangle (while resting it upright on the table). Slide the sanding sponge up and down until a cylinder shape is created.

9. To assemble the key: Apply glue to one end of the cylinder. Dip one of the flat balls into Foam Finish™ and pin it to the top of the cylinder. Add another flat disc to the first one (apply glue to the top of the other disc first). Repeat this process to add the semi-flattened ball, and then two more flat discs. Glue the flat side of the key lock to the opposite end of the cylinder. Allow this assembly to set up. Glue the carved key top to the last flat ball. Use straight pins to secure the key top. Allow the assembly to dry at least two hours. Be sure to place something under the key top while the key is drying to keep it from separating.

10. Glue the wood buttons in the holes beside the keyhole. Use the ball end of the hammer on the face of the key plate to create a hammer metal texture.

11. Cover the surface of the key and plate with Foam Finish™ or joint compound. Alternate between using the craft stick and a paintbrush. Be sure to apply enough to cover the holes of the foam. Allow the project to dry until hardened.

12. Dry sand where needed. See Chapter 1 for more information on sanding foam. Apply a coat of clear sealer. Allow it to dry.

13. Apply a coat of Instant Iron to cover each project. Allow them to dry for 12 hours.

14. Apply a coat of Instant Rust. Allow the paint to react for a few hours. Apply another coat if desired. Wait 24 hours before adding any more coats. The more coats that are added, the more brown and red a piece will typically get.

15. Mount these "antiques" in the shadow box with hot glue.

Materials

- Craft foam sheet, ½" x 12" x 36"
- Craft foam block, 1" x 6" x 12"
- 5 craft foam balls, 1½" diameter
- Foam Finish™* or joint compound
- Instant Iron paint*
- Instant Rust paint*
- Clear sealer*
- 1" bristle paintbrush
- #12 flat paintbrush
- 2 wood buttons*, ½" diameter
- 16" x 20" shadow box*
- Wooden craft stick
- Flathead pins
- 10mm ball tip pins
- Shape cutter*
- Hot multi-tipped tool* with knife blade and straight tips.
- Ball peen hammer
- Fine grit sanding sponge or sandpaper
- Glue*
- Scissors*

* Used in this project: Beacon Hold the Foam! glue and Foam Finish™; Fiskars® Shape Cutter™ and Softtouch™ scissors; Walnut Hollow Creative Versa-tool™ and wood buttons; Modern Options Sophisticated Finishes paints and clear sealer; and Timeless Frames Collections shadow box.

Quick Tip

- Decorate the shadow box any way you like. The box comes apart. Here, I covered the back with fabric. I also chose to paint the matte and box that surrounds the art. You may choose to have a heavy matte cut for your box. Here, I painted the outside frame with a coat of Dunmore Cream (Benjamin Moore). You may also use Folk Art® paint in Linen. Finally, I applied Asphaltum (Folk Art®) with a dry bristle brush.

Flared Box Clock

The sides of this box gently flare out, but how? Foam doesn't bend, or does it? Read on to see how.

Level 2

Safety First!

- **Use goggles and a fume mask when working with the heated knife.**
- **Be sure to sit the tool on a proper stand. It gets very hot!**
- **Use pliers to tighten the tip if it comes loose.**

1. Attach the knife blade tip to the multi-tipped tool, and plug it in.

2. Use scissors to cut the pattern from the pattern sheet.

3. Pin the pattern to the ½" thick foam, using the short 10mm pins. Cut out the pattern with the heated knife blade.

4. Repeat Step 2 for another piece of foam.

5. Use the heated blade to cut out the following pieces from the ½" thick sheet: two 6" x 8¼" rectangles, one 5¾" x 6" rectangle, one 4" x 4" square, one 4" x 6" rectangle, one 2" x 4" rectangle, one 6¾" x 4¾" rectangle.

6. Unplug the heated tool. Once the tool is cool, remove the knife tip. Replace it with the straight tip and plug the tool back in.

7. Using the serrated knife, cut out one 6" x 8" rectangle from the 1" x 6" x 12" block.

8. Place the pattern back on one of the pieces from Steps 2 to 4. Burn a hole that is about ¼" in diameter where the dot is on the pattern.

9. Flatten the two 6" x 8¼" pieces until they are about ¼" thick. Be sure to flatten each piece evenly throughout. The pieces should now be somewhat flexible and able to follow the curve of the flared pieces. If a piece is not bending easily enough, hammer a little more at the area that needs to bend.

10. Apply the foam glue to one side of a flared piece (cut from the pattern). Attach one of the hammered pieces to the glued area. Insert several pins to hold the pieces together.

11. Glue and pin the other end of the hammered piece to the other flared piece to create three of the four sides of the box.

Materials

- Craft foam sheet, ½" x 12" x 36"
- Craft foam block, 1" x 6" x 12"
- Joint compound
- Acrylic paint, Linen and Burnt Umber*
- Brown paint*
- Glazing medium*
- 1" bristle brush
- 4 wood finials (for legs), 2" tall
- 4 wood carvings*, 2" x 2" square
- 1 wood carving*, 4¼ " x 4¼" square
- Clock movement for ⅜" thick face*
- Self-adhesive Roman numerals*
- Decorative knob*
- 1 yd. beaded trim, Celadon
- 1 yd. upholstery trim, Celadon
- Flathead pins
- 10mm ball tip pins
- Hot multi-tipped tool with knife blade and straight tips*
- Putty knife
- Rubber mallet or hammer
- Paper towels
- Acrylic ruler*
- Permanent marker
- Glue*, hot glue gun and glue sticks, serrated knife, scissors*

*Used in this project: Beacon Hold the Foam!™ glue; Fiskars® Softouch™ scissors and acrylic ruler; Walnut Hollow Creative Versa-tool™; Plaid Enterprises Folk Art® acrylic paints and glazing medium; and Walnut Hollow Classic Dimensions embossed wood, clock movement, and roman numerals.

- Instead of the stick-on numerals, try one of the clock faces (Bezels) from Walnut Hollow or wood numerals. Paint however you like!
- Try green paint with the glaze for a different look.
- Try amber beaded trim. It looks great with the Burnt Umber paint. Change the upholstery trim color to taupe to coordinate.
- You may finish the inside of the box like the outside. Simply apply a coat of joint compound then paint and glaze it.
- Check out the planter in the outdoor chapter (page 90). It is the same box with a different purpose.

12. Apply glue to the other end of each flared piece. Attach the last hammered piece with more pins.

13. Apply glue to the bottom of the narrow end. Attach the base for the box (5¾" x 6" piece) with more straight pins. The 6" sides will attach to the flared pieces. Now you have a flared box!

14. Insert a finial into each corner on the bottom of the box to position the legs. Remove them and set aside.

15. To create the lid: Glue and pin the 1" x 6¾" x 4¾" piece to the 1" x 6" x 8" piece. On the opposite side of the 6" x 8" piece, attach the ½" x 4" x 6" piece. Finally, attach the ½" x 2" x 4" piece on top of the 4" x 6" rectangle. The lip of the lid (the 6¾" x 4¾" piece) should fit just inside the box. Sand away some of the lid if necessary for a good fit.

16. Tap each edge of the box and lid lightly with the mallet to bevel.

17. Cover the surface of the box and lid with joint compound. Apply a very thick coat of the compound with your hands and the putty knife. Use a little water to smooth it. Do not apply compound to the holes where the finials will attach. Glue the finials (legs) to the bottom of the box. Allow the box and lid to sit for 24 hours or until completely hardened.

18. Hot glue two of the small square wood pieces to the front of the box. Attach the other small squares to each side. Glue the large square piece to the back of the box.

19. Apply a coat of Linen paint. Allow it to dry.

20. Antique the box. Mix one part Burnt Umber paint to one part Glazing Medium, and then apply it with a paintbrush. Immediately wipe and blot away the excess glaze. Be sure to get the glaze in the cracks.

21. Melt a hole that is about ¼" diameter in the center of the 4" x 4" piece of foam. Glue this piece to the inside of the box. Be sure to line up the holes.

22. Add the clock movement to the back of the 4" x 4" square. Remove all of the small parts from the shaft of the clock except for the large rubber washer. Insert the shaft through the holes. Glue the black plastic box to the 4" x 4" piece of foam.

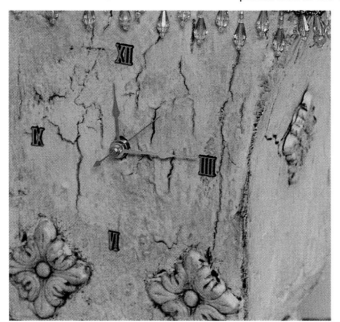

23. Attach the hands to the front of the clock. Follow the simple diagram on the back of the package.

24. Adhere the Roman numerals 3, 6, 8, and 12 to the front of the box. Move the hands to help position the numbers.

25. Using the hot glue gun, apply the beaded trim around the top lip of the box. Trim any excess. Apply the upholstery trim over the plain band on the beaded trim.

26. Glue the decorative knob to the top of the lid with foam glue.

Opposite: Note how the foam décor candlestick complements the Flared Box Clock.

Fleur-de-Lis Medallion

Enjoy this heavy-looking piece without ruining your walls!

Level 1

1. Use scissors to cut the pattern from the pattern sheet. Cut out the black circle in the center of the pattern.

2. Pin the pattern to the disc. Cut out the pattern with the coping saw (or serrated knife).

3. Cut out the hole in the center with a serrated knife. This cut does not have to be perfect. Start off by cutting an "X" shape in the circle, then slice from one section to the next, pushing the pieces through the back as they are cut. Remove the excess foam and use the emory board to smooth the edges. Dust off excess foam by rubbing with your fingers.

4. Use the pencil to score the shape of the two curved areas on each side and the thin lines that are on the inside of the pattern. Mark the four circles at the top of the pattern. Remove the pattern, and deepen the scored areas to about ¼" deep.

5. Use the potato peeler (or rotary tool) to carve the large moon shapes to ¼" deep. Refer to Chapter 1 for more information on carving.

6. To create indentations for the marbles to sit in: Push a marble deep into each circle that was marked in Step 4, then remove the marbles.

7. Use a scrap piece of foam and rub it along the edges of the wreath. This is only necessary on the inside of the wreath.

8. Slide the cut piece into the wreath from the back. If it does not fit yet, use a scrap piece of foam to sand the piece until it fits. Once it will fit snugly, apply glue at points where the piece will touch the wreath, then put the cut piece in place.

9. Cover the surface of the medallion with joint compound. Alternate between your hands, a pallet knife, and a paintbrush. Be sure to apply enough to cover the holes of the foam. Keep excess compound out of the areas where the marbles go. These holes really do not need the compound in them. Allow the project to dry until hardened.

10. Wet sand the piece again if necessary. Apply another coat of joint compound where holes are obvious. Allow the project to dry once more.

11. Apply a coat of clear sealer and allow it to dry.

12. Apply enough Instant Iron paint to cover the medallion. Allow it to dry for about 12 hours.

13. Apply a coat of Instant Rust. Allow the paint to react for a few hours. Apply another coat if desired. Wait 24 hours before adding any more coats. The more coats that are added, the more brown and red a piece will typically get.

14. Insert the marbles. If the hole is too large to hold them tight, use some clear-drying glue to secure them.

15. Create the hanger (see page 19). Insert the hanger wires up into the back of the medallion in the wreath. Apply glue to the insertion to secure. Allow the glue to dry before hanging the plaque.

Materials

- Craft foam disc, 16"
- Craft foam wreath, 18"
- Scrap piece of foam
- Joint compound
- Instant Iron paint*
- Instant Rust paint*
- Clear sealer*
- 1" bristle paintbrush
- #12 round paintbrush
- 4 marbles
- 10mm ball tip pins
- 6" of 18-gauge wire
- Coping saw
- Serrated knife
- Emory board
- Potato peeler or rotary tool
- Pallet knife
- Pencil, sandpaper, scissors*; disposable bowls
- * Used in this project: Fiskars® Softouch™ scissors; and Modern Options Sophisticated Finishes paints and sealer.

Doorway Arch

If you have ever wanted an arched doorway opening, this is the project for you! Inexpensive and easy, the doorway arch will dramatically impact any room.

Level 2

Safety First!

• **Wear eye protection while working with the rotary tool.**

Before you begin, read Quick Tips to see what thickness of foam to use. Purchase foam based on how deep your door opening is.

1. Cut out the pattern from the pattern sheet. Use the shape cutter to cut out the black areas on the pattern.

2. Pin the pattern to a 2" thick piece of foam. Pins will keep the pattern from curling while you work. Be sure to line up the pattern on two factory edges to get this first piece straight. Use the jigsaw or coping saw to cut around the outside of the pattern. Be sure to cut straight up and down. Do not angle the blade in the foam.

3. Use the rotary tool to carve the open areas of the pattern into the shape. Refer to Chapter 1 for instructions on using the rotary tool. The carved areas should finish at about ¾" deep.

4. Remove the pattern. Bevel the carved areas with the rotary tool and your fingers.

5. Flip the pattern over (backside up) and pin it down. Repeat Steps 2 to 4 for this piece of foam.

6. At this point, you should have two carved wedges. If you want the same pattern on the backside of each wedge, repeat this process for two more wedges on the same sheet of foam that you have been cutting from. If you want to create your own design for the other room, carve it into two more wedges at this time.

7. Place the pattern on the next sheet of foam. Cut out only the wedge shape with the jigsaw (or coping saw). Remove the pattern.

8. Flip the pattern over (backside up) and repeat Step 7 on the same sheet.

9. Assemble the wedges. Use glue to sandwich the pieces cut in Steps 7 and 8 between the 2" thick wedges that you have carved. Be sure the pieces line up with each other as closely as possible.

10. Square up the layers. Use a scrap piece of foam to sand any layers that are not lined up properly.

11. Reinforce the layers. Use greening pins to help hold the layers of foam together. Insert one prong of the pin into one layer and then the other prong into the other layer. Allow the glue to cure before continuing.

12. Cover each wedge with joint compound. First, apply the seam tape to the curved area of each wedge. It is not necessary to apply the seam tape to the straight sides. They will not show later. Apply joint compound, alternating between your hands, a putty knife, and a paintbrush. Be sure to apply enough to cover the layers of foam. You will want to make each wedge look as if it was carved from one large piece of material. Allow your piece to dry overnight or until hardened.

13. Wet sand the piece until any rough peaks are softened. Apply another coat of joint compound if the holes are still apparent. Some cracking occurs if you apply a thick coat of joint compound. This is not a problem if you do not mind the ancient look. If you want to get rid of the cracks, fill in with more joint compound.

14. Apply a coat of the Shenandoah Taupe paint. Allow the paint to dry.

Materials

- Craft foam sheets (see quick tips)
- Joint compound
- 1 qt. taupe paint-flat sheen*
- 1 qt. stone paint-flat sheen*
- 1" bristle brush
- #12 flat brush
- 2 boards, 2" x 4" x 8'
- Flathead pins
- Floral greening pins
- Disposable bowl
- Paper towels
- Jigsaw or coping saw
- Heavy-duty construction glue*
- 8' length of 2"x4" lumber
- Rotary tool*
- Shape cutter*
- Acrylic ruler* and cutting mat*

*Used in this project: Fiskars® Shape Cutter™, acrylic ruler, and cutting mat; Liquid Nails® for Heavy-Duty Construction glue; Dremel Multi-Pro rotary tool; and Benjamin Moore Shenandoah Taupe and Hot Spring Stones paints.

Quick Tip

- You will be cutting out the shape of the pattern several times on foam sheets, then you will stack and glue them to make a piece that is the depth of your doorway.
- 5" deep door opening: one 2" x 12" x 36" sheet and one 1" x 12" x 36" sheet
- 5½" deep door opening: one 2" x 12" x 36" sheet and one 1½" x 12" x 36" sheet
- 6" deep door opening: two 2" x 12" x 36" sheets
- Once installed, the arch is permanent. If you remove it, you will have to do drywall repair to the doorway, so be sure you like the carving! If not, find something that you will be able to commit to for a while.

- The wedges pictured were scaled to fit a five-foot wide opening. They are approximately 24" on the longer end. The wedges in our project are made ideally for a three-foot wide opening. However, you may use them in wider openings with success.
- Try adding wood pieces to embellish the wedges and save time.
- Try wallpaper or faux painting scrollwork on un-carved wedges.
- Instead of repeating the same carving on the backside of the arch, try a different design to coordinate with the adjoining room.

15. Antique the surface of each wedge with a mixture of one part Hot Springs Stones paint to one part water. Apply the thinned paint with a paintbrush. Immediately blot away excess paint with a paper towel. Allow the wedges to dry.

16. Use heavy-duty construction glue to attach each wedge on each side of the doorway opening. Apply a large bead of glue in a zigzag pattern on each straight side. Press one wedge firmly in the corner of the doorway. Hold for at least one minute. If possible, get a friend to continue holding the wedge while you install the other wedge. Do not worry if the wedge does not fit perfectly flush everywhere along the wall. Many houses do not have perfectly square openings. Fit them in the best way possible for now.

17. Repeat Step 16 for the other wedge.

18. Support the wedges overnight by placing a piece of lumber under each wedge at a diagonal. If the board will not rest properly on the other side of the door on the floor, place a chair where you need it.

19. After the wedges have sat overnight, remove the boards. If you did have a gap between the foam and the wall, fill it in with joint compound and allow it to dry. Touch up the areas with the same Taupe and Hot Springs Stones paint.

You have now changed the architecture of your room!

You do not have to commit to the same motif on both sides of the arch. The sun pictured is the backside of the scroll motif arch.

Gallery

Above: Here is an interesting idea! Foam décor may be used in low-traffic areas as wainscoting. This Baroque design may be a bit much for the beginner, so try something simple first.

Left: It takes some experience to complete this ancient-looking mask. If you have a wide window, such as the one shown here, try hanging the Oval Cartouche project (a much easier project to complete) in place of this mask.

Clockwise from top:
A different style of key
and plate balance the
other set you made.

What fun it is to play
with scale! The larger
keys are created with the
same techniques as the
smaller project.

Take a closer look at this
key and you will find a
bearded man! The 24"
tall key is an excellent
companion to the
framed pieces.

Clockwise from left:
Foam décor also may be incorporated into accent moldings! Here, foam carved moldings are incorporated with real unpolished marble tiles. Notice how they blend perfectly! The decorative scroll is also foam. It is the exact same pattern and size as the French Scroll Sconce (carved on thinner foam).

A Medieval inspired masterpiece! The technique is the same as the Oval Cartouche and it is lighter than any expensive store bought piece.

Foam décor combines with a simple wood frame to create an impressive coffee table. The motif ties in with the foam décor items located on the fireplace.

CHAPTER 3

Contemporary Flair

If you need a console table with that Art Deco flavor or perhaps some unique pieces of functional contemporary art, then turn the pages! In this chapter, learn to make lighted foam décor and extremely curvy pieces. The gallery will surprise you with the first fountain in the book. Also, see how Art Nouveau, Art Deco, Contemporary, and Eastern influences blend with ease. Achieving this effect was no big secret. Just unify with color!

Suspended Art

Whether you hang them as sculptures or add floral materials, this project is a fun touch to an empty corner.

Level 1

1. Apply the foam glue to the end of a swag hook. Insert the hook into the center of the wide end of the cone. Allow the glue to dry.

2. Cover the cone with joint compound until the holes are covered. Use your hands and some water to smooth the texture. Allow the cone to dry.

3. Dry sand any rough areas.

4. Apply a coat of Tapestry Wine paint. Allow this to dry.

5. Twist about six 18" long pieces of plastic wrap lengthwise. Untwist the pieces and set them aside.

6. Mix one part Glazing Medium to one part Burnt Umber paint. Apply a coat of the mixture. Press a piece of plastic wrap on the paint. Immediately pull it off. Repeat this process for the entire cone. Allow the cone to dry.

7. Tear the handmade paper into random unstructured pieces.

8. Apply accents of handmade paper all over the cone until desired. Apply decoupage glue to the cone, and then press on pieces of handmade paper. Apply decoupage glue over the top of the handmade paper to seal it. Repeat this process for the entire cone.

9. While the decoupage glue is still tacky, pick up a pinch of copper pigment and sprinkle it on the cone. Lightly dust the entire cone.

10. Coil and bend the copper tubing or wire in any way you like, leaving a small bend at each end to attach to the swag hooks.

11. Install a swag hook into your ceiling where desired. Follow the directions on the package. Place one end of the copper tubing or wire on this hook. Place the other end on the hook that is on the cone.

Quick Tip

- The cones shown in the photo are 18" and 21" tall. The instructions are to make one 21" tall cone.
- If you are making more than one cone, repeat the steps for the additional cones.
- Once the hook is firmly set into the cone, use it to hang the cone while applying joint compound.

Variations

- Try mixing several sizes of cones together.
- Try different background colors and paper textures.
- You may use the shape cutter to cut out handmade paper shapes. Place a sheet of scrap paper between the cutter and the handmade paper to prevent tearing.
- Insert grasses or even peacock feathers into the top of the cone. Make small bunches of these items and wire wood floral picks on them. Finally, insert the wood picks into the top wide end of the cone.

Materials

- Craft foam cone (see Quick Tips)
- Joint compound
- Acrylic paint, Tapestry Wine and Burnt Umber*
- Glazing medium*
- Powder pigment, copper*
- Handmade paper, navy, mustard, plum, green
- Flexible copper tubing or wire
- 2 antique brass ceiling hooks
- Decoupage glue*
- Foam glue*
- Plastic wrap
- Sponge paintbrush
- * Used in this project: Plaid Enterprises Apple Barrel® paints, Folk Art® Glazing Medium, and Modge Podge® decoupage glue; Jacquard Pearl Ex Powder Pigment; and Beacon Hold the Foam!™ glue.

Deco Influence Console Table

Foam décor objects on a foam table. The seemingly unrelated objects are brought together once again with color.

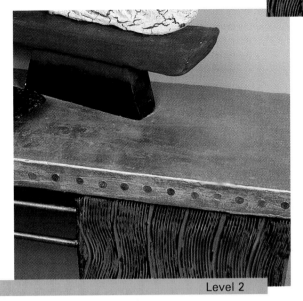

Level 2

1. To cut out the sides for the boxes (table base): Use a permanent marker to make marks on the end of a ½" thick sheet, 3" from each side. Mark the other end, 1½" from each side. Using the yardstick, connect the marks from one end to the other, creating two diagonals. Trace the lines with the permanent marker. Cut the lines with the knife or heated tool. See Chapter 1 for more on how to cut foam with either tool. It is important to slice through the foam straight, or the piece will not fit together properly. Repeat this step for the other three ½" thick sheets of foam.

2. Make marks on the end of a 1" thick sheet, 3½" from each side. Mark the other end, 4" from each side. Use the yardstick and connect the marks as in Step 1. Repeat this step for the other three 1" thick sheets of foam. Cut each piece as in Step 1.

3. Cut the 1" x 6" x 12" block in half.

4. To assemble a pedestal: Apply glue to one side of a 1" thick piece. Pin a ½" thick piece along the glued edge. Apply glue to one side of another 1" thick piece. Pin the other side of the first ½" thick piece. Add more glue to the other ends of the 1" thick foam sheets. Pin another ½" thick sheet. Glue a 6" x 6" piece to the narrow end of the box you just made. Set aside.

5. Repeat Step 4 to assemble another pedestal.

6. Cover each box with a layer of joint compound. Apply with your hands and some water to smooth it. Allow the compound to dry. It is not necessary to apply the compound to the bottom. Apply a coat of compound to the 2" thick sheet of foam.

7. When the boxes are dry, apply another coat of joint compound. Create texture on the boxes with the combing tool. Comb the boxes in a vertical wavy pattern. Allow the boxes to dry once more, and then apply a coat of joint compound to the bottom of the 2" thick sheet.

8. Once all the pieces are dry, paint them. Apply a coat of Red Primer to each box. Next, apply the Champagne Silver paint to the 2" thick sheet and the dowels. Allow the pieces to dry.

Materials

- 4 craft foam sheets, 1" x 12" x 36"
- 4 craft foam sheets, ½" x 12" x 36"
- 1 craft foam sheet, 2" x 12" x 36"
- 1 craft foam block, 1" x 6" x 12"
- Joint compound
- Putty knife
- Champagne silver spray paint*
- Red primer spray*
- Dark walnut wood stain*
- 3" paint roller and tray
- Greening pins
- 4 wood dowels, ½" x 12"
- Galvanized roofing nails
- 2 bags pea gravel
- Combing tool*
- Yardstick
- Hot multi-tipped tool or serrated knife
- Heavy-duty construction glue*
- Caulking gun
- Permanent marker
- * Used in this project: Liquid Nails® for Heavy-Duty Construction glue; Design Master Modern Metals™ spray paint; Krylon Primer; Minwax stain; and Plaid Enterprises combing tool.

Quick Tip

- The table will hold weight. However, if you want to use it for food, have a glass shop cut a piece to fit the top.
- When moving the table, carry it by lifting the boxes, not the top. Have one person carry each leg.

Below: The technique for making the wavy sconces is applied to create a wavy lamp. The leaf motif on the paper is repeated in the foam carving. An icon in India and China, the Feitian Goddess adds movement to this vignette.

9. Roll the stain onto the raised areas of the boxes. Be sure to roll out excess paint from the roller before applying it to the boxes.

10. Push galvanized nails along the sides of the 2" thick sheet to get a sheet metal look.

11. Turn the boxes so the wide end is up. Pour one bag of gravel into each box.

12. Poke a starter hole 4" from the top of each box toward the front and backside. Poke two more holes in each box 2" from the top of each box directly above the other holes. Apply glue to the ends of the dowels. Insert them in the holes, and then join the boxes together.

13. Secure the dowels. Apply more glue to the dowels, and then add pieces of scrap foam to the dowels on the inside of each box.

14. Apply a bead of glue along the top of each box. Place the 2" sheet centered on the boxes. Sit books on top of the table for about three hours or until the glue sets up.

You have now created your very own Art Deco influenced table.

Wavy Wall Sconce

Create almost any shape with foam! These wavy sconces are really easy to make!

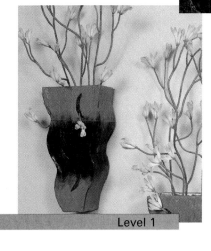

Level 1

Safety First!

- **Use goggles and a fume mask when working with the heated knife.**
- **Be sure to sit the tool on a proper stand. It gets very hot!**
- **Use pliers to tighten the tip if it comes loose.**

1. Attach the knife blade tip to the multi-tipped tool, and plug it in.

2. Use scissors to cut out the pattern from the pattern sheet.

3. Pin the pattern to the foam. Use the short 10mm pins. Score the foam where the black crescent areas are.

4. Cut around the pattern with the heated knife blade. Cut out the scored areas.

5. Repeat Steps 3 and 4 for another piece of foam. Using the heated blade, cut out two 4" x 12" pieces of foam.

6. Flatten the two pieces with a mallet until they are about ¼" thick. Be sure to flatten each piece evenly throughout. The piece should now be somewhat flexible and able to follow the curves of the wavy pieces. If the piece is not bending easily enough, hammer a little more at the areas that need to bend.

7. Apply glue to one of the ½" sides of a wavy piece. Attach one of the hammered pieces. Line up the flattened piece even with the wide end (top) of the wavy piece. Insert several greening pins along each side to hold the pieces together.

8. Attach the other end of the hammered piece from Step 7 to the other wavy piece. Apply glue to the end of the wavy piece before pinning.

9. Apply glue to the other end of each flared piece. Attach the last hammered piece with more pins.

10. Measure the length and width of the narrow end of the sconce. Cut a piece with these measurements from the ½" thick foam.

11. Apply glue to the bottom of the narrow end. Attach the piece from Step 10 with greening pins.

12. Cover the surface of the sconce with joint compound. Apply a coat of the compound with your hands and a putty knife. Use a small amount of water to smooth it. Allow the compound to dry.

13. Wet sand the sconce if needed. Apply another coat of joint compound if holes still show.

14. Stuff newspaper into the sconce. Spray on a coat of Red primer. Allow the paint to dry.

15. Squeeze some glass paint in the center of the sconce. Spread it around with your hands. Blot the paint with the sea sponge and paper towels. Spread some of the paint along the edges to highlight the curves. Allow the paint to dry. The paint will be somewhat transparent and shiny when dry.

16. Create the hanger (see page 19). Insert the hanger wires into the back of the sconce. Apply glue at the insertion to secure. Allow the glue to dry before hanging the sconce.

17. Cut the floral foam to fit inside the sconce. Stuff reindeer moss into the crescent openings. Pin it to secure. Pin more moss to the top of the foam to hide it. Insert your choice of artificial flowers. I have used Kangaroo Paw.

Materials

- Craft foam sheet*, ½" x 12" x 36"
- Joint compound
- Red primer spray*
- Glass paint, Cypress Green*
- Greening pins
- 6" length of 18-gauge florist wire
- 10mm ball tip pins
- Green reindeer moss
- Floral foam
- Flowers
- Sea sponge
- Disposable gloves
- Hot multi-tipped tool*
- Putty knife
- Rubber mallet
- Acrylic ruler
- Glue*, scissors*
- * Used in this project: Syndicate Sales Plastifoam® craft foam; Fiskars® Softouch™ scissors and acrylic ruler; Beacon Hold the Foam!™ glue; Krylon Primer spray; LeFranc & Bourgeois Glass paint; Walnut Hollow Creative Versatool™.

Variations

- If you want to use the sconce just as a decorative object on the wall, finish the inside of the box with joint compound.

Sunburst Curtain Rod

Create unique curtain rod finials from foam. Follow the simple steps to see how!

Level 1

Safety First!

- **Use goggles and a fume mask when working with the heated knife.**
- **Be sure to sit the tool on a proper stand. It gets very hot!**
- **Use pliers to tighten the tip if it comes loose.**

1. Attach the knife tip blade to the multi-tipped tool, and plug it in.

2. Use the shape cutter to cut out the pattern from the pattern sheet.

3. Pin the pattern to the foam. Cut around the pattern with the heated knife blade.

4. Repeat Step 3 for another finial.

5. Cover the surface of each finial with Foam Finish™ or joint compound. Alternate between the pallet knife and small paintbrush. Be sure to apply enough to cover the holes of the foam. Allow the project to dry until hardened.

6. Dry sand the finials if necessary. Use the emory board to get in the tight areas. Apply another coat of Foam Finish™ (or joint compound) if holes are still obvious. Allow the project to dry once more.

7. Apply the liquid adhesive with the small brush and foam paintbrush. Allow the adhesive to dry completely. It will become clear and very tacky to touch.

8. Rub the multi-color leafing flakes over the surface of the adhesive. Use cheesecloth to rub off the excess flakes. Use the emory board to get in the tight areas. Continue this process until the suns are smooth and all bits of flakes are gone.

9. If there are any areas that still show the white of the Foam Finish™, apply more adhesive and flakes.

10. Insert the piece of the sun that is not wavy into the end of a curtain rod. If the piece is too big, squeeze the piece and try it again. If it still will not fit into the end of the rod snugly, trim off small pieces with a knife until it fits. If you cut off too much, wrap some tissue paper around the piece to increase the size again.

Materials

- Craft foam sheet, ½" x 12" x 36"
- Foam Finish™* or joint compound
- Multi-color metal leafing flakes*
- Liquid leafing adhesive*
- 1" foam paintbrush
- #12 round paintbrush
- Cheese cloth
- 10mm ball tip pins
- Shape cutter*
- Hot multi-tipped tool with knife blade tip*
- Emory boards
- Pallet knife
- * Used in this project: Beacon Foam Finish™; Fiskars® Shape Cutter™; Walnut Hollow Creative Versa-tool™; and LeFranc & Bourgeois Kaleidoscope Metal Leafing Flakes and liquid adhesive.

Variations

- To get the look of the copper rod shown in the photo, purchase a ¾" round piece of copper tubing at a home store. You may have it cut to length at the store, so measure before you go! Also, purchase two wood curtain rod brackets and paint them with copper paint or cover them with copper leafing flakes.
- You can coordinate the finish to match any type of rod you may have.
- Try making scroll finials. The scroll finial in the first chapter (page 32) is easily made into a curtain finial. Make the wide base narrow enough to fit into the end of your rod.

Contemporary Flair

Illuminated Frames

Handmade paper is dramatically backlit, adding interest and texture.

Level 2

Safety First!
- **Use goggles and a fume mask when working with the heated knife.**
- **Be sure to sit the tool on a proper stand. It gets very hot!**
- **Use pliers to tighten the tip if it comes loose.**

1. Plug in the multi-tipped tool with a straight tip attached. Melt a path on the back of one of the frames for the light cord to come through.

2. Apply a coat of joint compound to the sides of this frame. Use your hands and some water to smooth the joint compound.

3. Cover the front and sides of the frame that was *not* used in Step 1. *Important: Do not get joint compound on the back of the frame.*

4. Once the first layer of compound has hardened, apply another coat to the *front* and *inside* of the frame that was *not* used in Step 1. Comb the joint compound in a wavy pattern. Allow the compound to dry completely.

5. Spray a coat of the Metallic Taupe paint on the front side of the frame from Step 3 and 4. Allow the paint to dry.

6. Flip the frame that is wavy textured so that the backside faces up. Lay the handmade paper on the frame opening. Pin the paper to the frame with several straight pins. Pull the paper as tight as possible.

7. Apply a bead of glue along the center of the frame from the previous step. Press the other frame on top of this one. Be sure that the melted area (from Step 1) is on the back of the assembly (it will be to the wall). If you did get some joint compound on the backs of the frames, sand it off before gluing the frames together.

8. Let the glued pieces sit for about two hours. Place heavy books on top of the pieces so they do not separate.

9. Apply joint compound to the outer sides of the glued pieces. First, cover the crack where the pieces meet with joint compound. Next, apply joint compound as in Step 4. Comb to texture the sides. Allow the compound to dry completely.

10. Spray a coat of Metallic Taupe paint on the sides. Place a piece of newspaper over the frame opening to protect the paper from over-spray. Allow the paint to dry.

11. Add the Christmas lights. Keep the lights in the plastic tray they came in. Most of the trays will fit snugly in the frame opening. If the lights do not fit, wrap them around a piece of craft foam, and then insert that into the opening.

12. Feed the cord through the channel made in Step 1.

13. Create two hangers (see page 19). Insert the hanger wires into the back of the frame. Apply glue to the insertion to secure. Allow the glue to dry before hanging your frame. You may hang your creation either horizontally or vertically.

Materials
- 2 craft foam rectangle frames, 12" x 17"
- Joint compound
- Metallic taupe spray paint*
- Marbleized handmade paper*, 11" x 14"
- Flathead pins
- 1 strand of 50 or 100 Christmas lights
- Two 6' lengths 18-gauge wire
- Hot multi-tipped tool with straight tip*
- Wire cutters
- Combing tool*
- Heavy-duty construction glue*

For Optional Steps:
- ½" copper elbows for any bends in the pipes
- ½" diameter copper pipe
- Copper pipe hangers
- Extension cord
- Electrical plug
- Black electrical tape
- Wire cutters
- Matte knife
- Hot glue gun and glue sticks
- Tube cutter (optional)
* Used in this project: Design Master Modern Metals™ spray paint; Black Ink™ handmade paper; Plaid Enterprises combing tool; Liquid Nails® for Heavy-Duty Construction glue; and Walnut Hollow Versa-tool™ creative heat tool.

- The frames are 2" thick blocks with pre-made openings. If you cannot find them in your area, purchase a 2" x 12" x 36" sheet of foam. Cut two blocks that are 12" x 17". Mark two inches all the way around to the inside. Use a jigsaw or serrated knife to cut out the centers. Sand with a scrap piece of foam.
- If you are making more than one frame, repeat the steps for the additional frames.
- You could also comb the joint compound with a hair clipper comb or wide tooth hair pick. Try various items around the house to create textures.

14. Hang the frame with appropriate wall anchors. Add an extension cord, if needed, and plug in the lights. You will see the colors in the paper glow. Let there be light!

Optional Steps:

So you do not want to see a cord hanging down on the wall? Go for the hot industrial look!

1. Draw a diagram to see how you want the copper to bend.

2. Measure how long you want the pipe pieces to be.

3. Go to a home store with your diagram. Have a store employee cut the straight pipe for you in the lengths you need.

4. When you return home, hang the frame where it needs to be. Plug the lights in the extension cord. Tuck these plugs in the back of the frame. Feed the cord through the channel. Plug in the extension cord to make sure the lights are working, and then unplug the cord. Remove the frame from the wall.

5. Cut off the plug on the extension cord and assemble the pipes. Lay out all of the pipe pieces and the frame as in your diagram. Feed the cord through each piece before attaching them to each other. Once the cord is running through all the pieces, join the pieces together. If the pieces fit loosely, apply hot glue to one piece, then insert it into the other. This is fine since the pipes are not for water. If the elbow seems too small to fit on the pipe, try twisting it a little. It will fit with some patience.

6. Add a new plug to the severed extension cord. Follow the directions on the plug package. *Tip: When you purchase the items for this project, take the extension cord and new plug to the electrical area of the store. Strip the plug from the cord at the store so you can see what the wires look like. Ask the electrical expert which wire is which in comparison to the plug instructions. This way, you do not have to guess which one is the ground wire and which is the hot wire later. Do not put the plug on at the store though—it defeats the purpose!*

7. Once all the pieces are joined securely, grab a friend and bring the whole assembly to the wall. Hang the frame back on the wall. Use the pipe hangers to attach the pipes to the wall.

8. Plug in the newly wired plug and the lights should shine! If not, check your wiring.

Gallery

Left: Inspired by Art Nouveau ironwork, this piece is warmed up with a great copper finish. The copper color also ties in with the ceiling molding. Cross-linking your foam décor project with other colors in the room creates a cohesive feel.

Below: Foam décor with water! This fountain features rippling water and a bronze finish. This is no more than a foam sheet and several stacked wreaths. The box shows how simple foam décor can be! Create a box and cover it with fabric. You may glue or sew it on. How easy is that?

Contemporary Flair

CHAPTER 4

Garden Gathering

The mood is set for an enchanted garden gathering. Sounds of water flowing, ambient lighting, and opulent flowers invite guests to stay for an enchanted evening! This chapter of *Foam Décor* has all of this covered.

Whimsical Sundial

A unique focal point for any garden!

Level 2

- **Use goggles and a fume mask when working with the heated knife.**
- **Be sure to sit the tool on a proper stand. It gets very hot!**
- **Use pliers to tighten the tip if it comes loose.**

1. Insert the knife blade tip into the multi-tipped tool and plug it in.

2. To cut out the sides for the pyramid-shaped part of the sundial: Make marks on the end of a ½" thick sheet, 3" from each side. Mark the other end, 1½" from each side. Using the yardstick, connect the marks from one end to the other, creating two diagonals. Mark off the lines with the permanent marker. Use the heated blade or serrated knife to cut through the marks. See Chapter 1 for instructions on using the hot multi-tipped tool. It is important to slice through the foam straight, or the piece will not fit together properly.

3. Make marks on the end of a 1" thick sheet, 3½" from each side. Mark the other end, 4" from each side. Use the yardstick and connect the marks as in Step 2. Cut each piece as in Step 2.

4. To assemble the flattop pyramid: Apply glue to one side of a 1" thick piece. Pin a ½" thick piece along the glued edge. Apply glue to one side of another 1" thick piece. Pin to the other side of the first ½" thick piece. Add more glue to the other ends of the 1" thick foam sheets. Pin another ½" thick sheet to these. Set aside.

5. Measure the wide end of the box. It should be approximately 9" x 9". Use the heated tool to cut a piece that fits the measurement. Dry fit the piece on the box. Adjust the size of the block if necessary. Apply a bead of glue to the bottom of the box and attach the cut piece with greening pins.

6. To create the legs: Use the heated tool (or a serrated knife) to carve two of each leg pattern piece from the remaining portion of 1" thick foam. Use the pencil to score the scrolls. Carve the scroll deeper into the foam with the pencil, once the pattern is removed.

7. Glue the scroll foot pieces to the opposite sides of the box bottom. Glue the other two cut pieces on the remaining sides. Secure with greening pins. Allow the glue to cure for about two hours.

8. Cut out the triangle pattern from a ½" thick scrap of foam. You may use any of the cutting tools to do this.

9. Exchange the heated tool knife blade tip for the straight tip. Be sure not to touch the hot tool or tips!

10. While the glue cures, melt the decoration into each side of the box. Lay the box on its side while doing this step. Draw scrolling N, S, E, and W letters on the box with permanent marker to show the directions. Draw a half circle and waves at the bottom of each side, as pictured. Use the heated tool to melt each design into the box.

11. Sit one bag of pea gravel (or play sand) inside the hollow box to keep the sundial from blowing away. If you live in a windy area, more gravel may be needed.

12. Divide the disc into four even sections. Melt lines into the disc to show 3, 6, 9, and 12 o'clock.

13. Place the taller side of the triangle in the center of the disc. Point the shorter end directly at one of the marks made in Step 10. Glue the triangle in place.

14. Apply glue to the narrow end of the box. Position the disc so that the long side of the triangle faces directly North.

15. Cover the sundial with a layer of joint compound. Apply it with your hands and some water to smooth it. Allow the compound to dry. You do not need to apply any joint compound down in the shallow carved areas.

16. Once the sundial is dry, spray the Faux Stone paint all over the project in a random manner, alternating the colors of paint. Allow the paint to dry completely.

17. Antique the sundial. Mix one part Olive Green paint to one part glazing medium, and then apply the glaze with a paintbrush. Immediately blot away excess paint with paper towels. Apply more paint on the North side and less on the South. The lower carved areas should have more paint in them. This will give the effect of moss growing in the cracks.

18. Apply two coats of the clear sealer. Follow directions on the can. Allow the last coat to cure before placing the sundial in your garden.

Materials

- 3 craft foam sheets, 1" x 12" x 36"
- 2 craft foam sheets, ½" x 12" x 36"
- 1 craft foam disc, 1" x 16"
- Joint compound
- Faux stone paint, Charcoal Sand and Black Granite*
- Acrylic paint, Olive Green Dark*
- Glazing medium*
- 1 qt. brush-on clear outdoor sealant*
- Paintbrush
- Greening pins
- 1 bag pea gravel or play sand
- Hot multi-tipped tool with knife blade and straight tips*
- Caulking gun
- Heavy-duty construction glue*
- Yardstick
- Paper towels
- Permanent marker
- * Used in this project: Krylon Make It Stone® paint; Plaid Enterprises Folk Art® acrylic paint and Glazing Medium; Minwax Helmsman Outdoor Spar Urethane; Liquid Nails for Heavy-Duty Construction glue; and the Walnut Hollow Creative Versa-tool™.

Stamped Ornament

It does not get easier than this! This one is as easy as cover, paint, and stamp!

1. Insert the skewer into the foam ball.

2. Cover the ball with a coat of Foam Finish™ or joint compound. Apply it with your hands and turn the ball until it is covered. Place the ball on the skewer to dry.

3. Dry sand the ball if needed.

4. Apply Linen paint to the ball with the foam brush. Let it dry.

5. Paint Antiquing Medium onto the stamp. Blot the stamp on a paper plate, and then apply it to the ball. Gently press the stamp first in the center, and then rock it to each side to get the image on the curved surface. Repeat this process for the entire ball.

6. Apply two coats of clear sealer if using outdoors.

7. Enjoy decorative orbs for nearly no money at all!

Materials

- Craft foam ball, 6" diameter
- 2" thick scrap piece of foam
- Foam Finish™ or joint compound
- Acrylic paint, Linen*
- Antiquing medium, Apple Butter Brown*
- #12 flat paintbrush
- 1" foam paintbrush
- 2" Fleur-de-Lis sponge stamp*
- Paper plate
- Bamboo skewer
- Clear sealer
- * Used in this project: Plaid Enterprises Folk Art® paint and antiquing medium; Anita's Chunky Stamps; Beacon Foam Finish™.

Quick Tip

- Use pillar candleholders to display the balls.
- Create the small green ball (shown in the bowl). Glue chunks of green mood moss to a 3" ball.

Variations

- Make several sizes of balls to make a group. Try different stamps on each one for a change.

Scroll Ornament

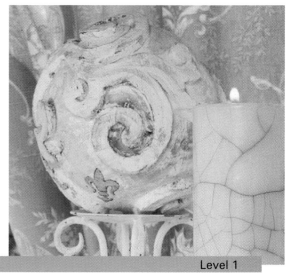

The illusion of relief carving without the difficulty! Make several and group them!

Safety First!

- **Use goggles and a fume mask when working with the heated knife.**
- **Be sure to sit the tool on a proper stand. It gets very hot!**
- **Use pliers to tighten the tip if it comes loose.**

Level 1

1. Plug in the multi-tipped tool with the blade tip on it. Insert the skewer into the foam ball.

2. Cover the ball with Foam Finish™ (or joint compound). Use your hands to spread it around. Place the ball on the skewer to dry.

3. Cut out the scroll pattern from the pattern sheet with the shape cutter.

4. Cut out four of the scroll pattern from the ½" thick foam. Use 10mm ball pins to hold the pattern in place. If you do not want to keep pinning, trace the pattern four times onto the foam with a permanent marker.

5. Run the permanent marker along all of the cut edges to soften them.

6. Gently pound each cut piece of foam with the flat side of the hammer right side up. Turn each piece over and tap each piece with the ball tip end of the hammer. Each piece will be about ¼" thick when you are finished.

7. If the ball is dry, sand it to smooth any rough areas.

8. Glue and pin the scrolls to the ball. Cut some of the scrolls apart to help with fit, if desired. Some pieces may crack a little; this may be fixed with Foam Finish™ (or joint compound) later.

9. Cover the scrolls with Foam Finish™. Use the paintbrush to help spread it. Allow the coating to dry. Apply a second coat if the holes and/or cracks are still apparent.

10. Apply Linen paint to the ball. Allow the paint to dry.

11. Apply the antiquing medium to the ball with the paintbrush. Blot away excess medium with paper towels.

12. Use the stamp to decorate any open areas. Paint antiquing medium onto the stamp. Blot the stamp on a paper plate, then apply it to the ball. Be sure to gently press the stamp first in the center, then rock it to each side to get the image on the curved surface.

Materials

- Craft foam ball, 6" diameter
- Craft foam sheet, ½" x 12" x 36"
- 2" thick scrap piece of foam
- Foam Finish™ or joint compound
- Acrylic paint, Linen*
- Antiquing medium, Apple Butter Brown*
- Clear outdoor sealer*
- #12 flat paintbrush
- 2" Fleur-de-Lis sponge stamp*
- bamboo skewer or small dowel
- Flathead pins
- 10mm ball pins OR permanent marker
- Shape cutter* and self-healing mat
- Hot multi-tipped tool
- Ball-peen hammer
- Pallet knife
- Paper towels
- Glue*

* Used in this project: Fiskars® Shape Cutter™ and cutting mat; Plaid Enterprises Folk Art® paint and antiquing medium; Anita's Chunky Stamps; Beacon Hold the Foam! glue and Foam Finish™, Walnut Hollow Creative Versa-Tool; and Minwax Helmsman Spar Urethane.

Variations

- Create several sizes of balls with the same pattern. Cut out more scrolls for larger balls.

Garden Party Lights

Level 1

Party late into the evening with foam décor lighting the way! These lights provide plenty of light so that guests will not trip over each other.

- **Use goggles and a fume mask when working with the heated knife.**
- **Be sure to sit the tool on a proper stand. It gets very hot!**
- **Use pliers to tighten the tip if it comes loose.**

1. Plug in the multi-tipped tool with the straight tip attached to it.

2. Melt a hole in each cup, about 1" around. Be sure to wear the fume mask! Use the paper edgers to remove the thick lip from each cup.

3. Punch three diamonds into the sides of each cup. Slide the paper punch onto the cup. Place the piece of wood under the paper punch. Punch the diamond through the cup. Use both hands and push firmly. Repeat this process for two more diamonds per cup. Save the punched diamonds.

4. Attach the paintbrush to the Mossy Green paint. Apply vertical strokes of paint to the outside of each cup. Only one coat is needed. The streaking effect the paint makes on the foam cups makes them look like stained glass when lit. Set each one on newspaper to dry. Rinse the paintbrush when finished to use again.

5. In a disposable bowl, mix the Deep Purple paint with White. Use the craft stick to stir until the colors are thoroughly blended. Use the funnel to pour some of the paint back into either empty bottle. Save the extra paint.

6. Attach the paintbrush to the bottle and paint each cut diamond with the new purple color. Set the diamonds on newspaper to dry.

7. Once the diamonds are dry, use the glue to attach the purple diamonds where shown in the photo. Allow the glue to dry.

8. Attach the cups to the Christmas lights. Unscrew a bulb from the strand. Insert the socket through the hole in the cup. Screw the light back on the strand. Repeat this step for the rest of the lights and cups.

9. Wrap the floral garland around the cord between the lights to disguise it.

10. Hang your romantic outdoor lights and enjoy them anytime!

Materials

- 50 foam cups, 16 oz.
- 1 strand clear outdoor Christmas lights, 50 ct.
- 6 garlands, 9 feet each
- Outdoor acrylic enamel, Mossy Green, Deep Purple, and White*
- 1" screw-on paintbrush (fits on the paint bottle)*
- Diamond motif paper punch*
- Disposable bowl
- Craft stick or Popsicle stick
- Newspapers
- Funnel (optional)
- Hot multi-tipped tool with straight tip*
- Paper edgers*
- Glue*
- * Used in the project: Plaid Enterprises Outdoor Gloss acrylic enamel and paint bottle brush; Emagination Crafts paper punch; Fiskars®, Paper Edgers (Provincial); Beacon Hold the Foam! glue, and Walnut Hollow Creative Versa-Tool.

Quick Tip

- Measure how many strands of light you will need before going out to purchase supplies.
- You may stretch the garland coverage by wrapping it around the cord fewer times.

Variations

- You may add beaded trim to each cup for added sparkle. Purchase pre-beaded trim. Clip off a strand and immediately hot-glue it to the cup. Usually, beaded trim has different lengths on the strand. Be sure to use the same lengths of bead on a cup to keep it balanced. If you need to stop while doing this step, put a piece of tape at the end of the cut trim so the beads do not unravel.
- There are an infinite number of combinations of Paper Edgers and punches you could use for this project. Customize to your theme! It is best to choose punches that do not have a lot of tiny areas. Detailed filigree corners and lace patterns do not punch through easily.

Weathered Crackle Window

Add a touch of architecture. Create a window where there wasn't one.

Level 1

- **Wear eye protection while working with cutting tools**.

1. Make a pattern. Mark a 4" x 7" rectangle on a piece of paper. Cut out the rectangle.

2. Cut out the scroll pattern from the pattern sheet with the shape cutter. Set aside.

3. Place the rectangle pattern on the 1" x 12" x 36" sheet. Use a permanent marker to trace around the pattern eight times. Refer to the photo for placement.

4. Cut the 16" wreath in half. Place the inside opening of the half-wreath on the top edge of the sheet. Mark the arch with a permanent marker.

5. Make the arched window openings. With a permanent marker, add an arch shape to the top two rectangles. Follow the shape of the arch that is already drawn.

6. Use the jigsaw or serrated knife to cut out all of the window openings. Use scrap pieces of foam to sand any rough cuts. Cut the arch at the top of the sheet at this time as well.

7. Glue the wreath to the arched top of the sheet. Sand if necessary to get a good fit. The back of the wreath and the sheet should both be laying flat on the work surface.

8. Pin the scroll pattern to the 1" x 12" x 12" block of foam. Cut out the pattern. You may get cleaner cuts if you use a heated multi-tipped tool (with a knife blade) to score the pattern. Then use a serrated knife to finish the cuts.

9. Repeat Step 8 for another scroll.

10. Glue and pin the scrolls to the top of the wreath. Place them in the center.

11. Cover the window assembly with joint compound. Wet sand after two hours. See Chapter 1 for information on how to apply the compound Allow it to dry. *Important: Since you will be using spray paint that may eat away foam, be sure to cover the holes of the foam completely.*

12. While the window assembly dries, flatten one end of each ball. Apply joint compound to the two balls. Roll the ball in your hand with some water to spread the compound. Set aside to dry.

13. Once the joint compound has hardened, dry sand any rough areas.

14. Glue the balls to the ends of the wreath. Glue the finial to the center of the scrolls.

15. Cover the window with a coat of Ivory Crackle base coat. Allow the base coat to dry at least one hour before applying the topcoat. Read the can for more about spraying techniques. *Note: Most spray paints are not made for craft foam. However, since you are completely covering the foam, the paint will not harm the foam.*

16. Apply the Billiard Green top coat. Allow the paint to dry before proceeding.

17. Turn the window backside up. Pin one sheet of vellum behind each opening.

18. Create a hanger (see page 19). Insert the hanger wires into the back of the wreath. Apply glue to the insertion to secure. Allow the glue to dry before hanging.

Materials

- Craft foam wreath, 16" diameter x 2" face x 2" thick
- Craft foam block, 1" x 12" x 12"
- Craft foam sheet, 1" x 12" x 36"
- 2 craft foam balls, 2" diameter
- Joint compound
- Weathered Crackle base coat, Ivory*
- Weathered Crackle top coat, Billiard Green*
- #12 round paintbrush
- Wood finial, 2" tall
- 4 sheets velum paper, Fern pattern*, 8½" x 11"
- Sheet of paper, 8½" x 11"
- Flattop straight pins
- 1" putty knife
- 6" length 18-gauge florist wire
- Jigsaw (optional)
- Shape Cutter*
- Serrated knife
- Glue*
- Permanent marker
- * Used in this project: Beacon Hold the Foam!™ glue, Fiskars® Shape Cutter™ and printed vellum; and Valspar Weathered Crackle products.

Quick Tip

- You do not have to use a jigsaw. The serrated knife will work for this project. The jigsaw is just a time saver.
- You may use a heated tool to cut out the pieces. You will need to finish them off with a serrated knife, as the blades do not cut all the way through 1" thick foam.

Variations

- This project, as shown, is meant to be in a covered area. It cannot sit in the rain because the vellum will wrinkle. However, you may weatherproof the project. First, do not use vellum. Leave the openings without a backing. After you follow all of the steps above, apply a waterproofing sealer such as Minwax Helmsman Spar Urethane.

Garden Statue

Every garden patio needs statues.
Here are two easy and elegant ideas!

Level 1

Safety First!

- **Safety comes first. Use goggles and a fume mask when working with the heated knife.**
- **Be sure to sit the heated tool on a proper stand.**
- **Use pliers to tighten the tip if it comes loose.**

1. Plug in the multi-tipped tool with the knife blade attached to it.

2. Cut the following square pieces from the ½" sheet of foam: one 6" x 6", one 5½" x 5½", and one 2" x 2". Refer to Chapter 1 for instructions on using the heated tool.

3. Use the 10mm pins to hold the pattern on the ½" thick foam sheet. Cut four of the pattern piece with the heated tool (or the serrated knife).

4. To assemble the box: Refer to Fig. 8. Join the pattern pieces to make a box. Note how the sides come together. Put glue on each piece as you assemble the box. Secure with straight pins.

5. Glue the smaller 5½" square on top of the 6"square. Glue the box assembly to the stacked squares. Glue the 2" square to the top of the box.
Optional: If you will be using this statue outside, allow the glue to dry for two hours. Pour pea gravel inside the hollow box to weigh it down.

Side 2 · Side 1 · Side 3 · Side 4

Fig. 8

6. Make a hole for the finial to fit in the center of the 2" square. Remove the finial.

7. Cover the surface of the box with Foam Finish™ (or joint compound). Alternate between the pallet knife and a paintbrush. Be sure to apply enough to cover the holes of the foam. Allow the project to dry until hardened.

8. Wet sand the project if necessary. Apply another coat of Foam Finish™ (or joint compound) if foam holes can still be seen. Allow the project to dry once more.

9. Apply a coat of Canyon Shadow Millstone paint. Allow it to dry.

10. Meanwhile, paint the finial and buttons with the Boulder paint.

11. After the Canyon Shadow paint is dry, place the stencil on one side of the box. The stencil will run off the sides toward the top. Spray the stencil with Boulder paint. Repeat this process for the other three sides.

12. Glue the finial to the top, and glue one button to the bottom of the base in each corner.

Variations

- You may increase or decrease the size of the pattern and squares to create a group of statues that are varied in size.

Materials

- Craft foam sheet, ½" x 12" x 36"
- Foam Finish™* or joint compound
- Millstone spray paint, Boulder and Canyon Shadow*
- #12 flat paintbrush
- 4 wood buttons*, ½" diameter
- Wood finial, 2" tall
- Flat-head straight pins
- 10mm ball tip pins
- Victorian Swirl stencil*
- Pea gravel (optional)
- Hot multi-tipped tool* or serrated knife
- Small putty knife
- Hammer (optional)
- Permanent marker
- Glue*, ruler*
- * Used in this project: Fiskars® acrylic ruler; Beacon Hold the Foam!™ glue and Foam Finish™; StenSource® International stencil; Walnut Hollow wood buttons and Creative Versa-Tool; and Valspar Textured Millstone spray paint.

Garden Finial

An elegant finial is the perfect companion for the garden statue.

Level 1

1. Square off the sides of the cone. Use a pipe saw (or serrated knife) and shave the cone at an angle. Create four "sides." Once four sides have been roughly cut, sand them with a scrap piece of foam.

2. Score a line around the four-sided cone, about ½" from the base. Deepen this line with the pencil and potato peeler. See the detail in the picture. This is the notched area.

3. Flatten the top and bottom of the ball by shaving it with the saw (or serrated knife). Pound it on a table to flatten it more. You may also use a hammer.

4. To assemble the finial: Break the craft stick in half. Insert one piece into the center of the square block. Add glue to the end of the stick, and attach the flattened ball. Insert the other piece of craft stick into the top of the ball. Add glue, then position the squared cone.

5. Cover the surface of the finial with Foam Finish™ or joint compound. Alternate between the pallet knife and a paintbrush. Be sure to apply enough to cover the holes of the foam. Allow the project to dry until hardened.

6. Wet sand the project if necessary. Apply another coat of Foam Finish™ (or joint compound) if foam holes can still be seen. Allow the project to dry once more.

7. Apply a coat of Boulder paint. Allow it to dry.

8. Accent the cracks in the finial by painting on Olive Green Dark paint. Wipe and blot the paint immediately to soften the color. Allow it to dry once again.

Materials

- Craft foam cone, 4" x 9"
- Craft foam block, 2" x 4" x 4"
- Craft foam ball, 4" diameter
- Foam Finish™* or joint compound
- Millstone spray paint, Boulder*
- Acrylic paint, Olive Green Dark*
- #12 flat paintbrush
- Paper towels
- Craft stick
- Pipe saw or serrated knife
- Pallet knife
- Potato peeler
- Hammer (optional)
- Glue*, pencil
- * Used in this project: Beacon Foam Hold the Foam!® glue and Foam Finish™; Valspar Textured Millstone spray paint; and Plaid Enterprises Folk Art®, acrylic paint.

Variations

- You may adjust the sizes of all the shapes used proportionately to create a larger or smaller finial.

Bird Bath and Feeder

Separate components allow you to easily disassemble for winter without straining your back!

Level 2

- **Always be aware of where your hands are when working with a jigsaw or any saw. Do not place fingers in front of the blade at any time. Do not wear loose clothing, as it may get caught in the blade.**
- **Wear safety glasses when working with a jigsaw**
- **Wear a fume mask while mixing powdered grout.**

1. Measure several times from the bottom of the cylinder up to 26". Mark around the cylinder and connect the lines. Have a friend help hold the tube still while you cut the tube. Be sure the friend wears safety glasses, too!

2. To assemble the base: Apply glue to a 16" disc. Attach it to the bottom of the 16" wreath. Insert greening pins through the bottom of the disc. Glue the 14" wreath on top of the 16" wreath. Glue a 12" wreath on top of the 14" wreath. Set aside.

3. To assemble the bowl: Place the 18" ring on top of the insulation foam. Trace around the wreath with a permanent marker. Remove the wreath, and cut the circle from the insulation foam with the jigsaw (or coping saw). Glue the insulation foam to the bottom of the 18" wreath. Leave the assembly bottom-side up. Glue the other 16" disc to these pieces. Glue the bottom side of the second 12" wreath to the 16" disc.

4. Apply heavy-duty construction glue to the inside seam of the bowl. Allow glue to dry until hardened. Pour water into the bowl to test for leaks. Repair any leaks with more construction glue.

5. Assemble the floating feeder. Glue the 4" disc to the bottom of the 6" wreath.

6. Cover the base with tile grout. Mix the grout according to the package directions. Mix in the additive instead of water to make it weatherproof and help keep it from cracking. Apply the mixture to all of the parts of the base that will be seen. Use a combination of the putty knife and your hands (wear the gloves).

7. Cover the bowl and feeder with the grout mixture in the same manner as Step 6.

8. Cover the cement forming tube with more grout. Let all parts of the birdbath cure before proceeding. Follow the grout manufacturer's instructions.

9. Wet the sea sponge and squeeze out excess water. Squeeze Mossy Green paint onto a paper plate. Dip the sponge in the paint and wipe it onto the birdbath. Wipe and blot excess paint with paper towels. Allow the paint to dry.

10. Place the tube in the base. Sit the bags of pea gravel or play sand in the base and in the tube. Sit the bowl on top of the tube.

11. Add water after the grout is fully cured. Float the feeder with some birdseed in it. You may also pin the feeder to the side of the bowl, if desired.

Quick Tip

- Heavy-duty construction glue is preferred for both gluing and sealing seams. Allow it to cure before covering.
- If you purchase a full sheet of insulation foam, you will have enough left to make the Fabulous Floor Fountain!
- Mix grout in small batches because it hardens quickly. Divide the box or bag of grout additive accordingly.

Materials

- 2 craft foam wreaths, 2" x 2" x 12"
- Craft foam wreath, 2" x 2" x 14"
- Craft foam wreath, 2" x 2" x 16"
- Craft foam wreath, 2" x 2" x 18"
- 2 craft foam discs, 1" x 16"
- Craft foam disc, 1" x 4"
- Craft foam wreath, 6" diameter
- Insulation foam, ½" x 18" x 18"
- Water-submersible caulk
- Cardboard concrete forming tube, approx. 12" diameter
- Tile grout and acrylic additive
- Outdoor acrylic enamel, Mossy Green*
- Greening pins
- Sea sponge
- Paper plate
- 2 bags pea gravel or play sand
- Jigsaw or coping saw
- Putty knife
- Disposable gloves
- Paper towels
- Heavy-duty construction glue*
- Yardstick
- Permanent marker
- * Used in this project: Liquid Nails® for Heavy-Duty Constructions glue; and Plaid Enterprises Outdoor Gloss® acrylic enamel.

Variations

- You may cover your birdbath with either joint compound (plus one coat of basement waterproofing paint) or tile grout. Tile grout is really great for most outdoor foam projects because it saves waterproofing steps later. Beware, the grout will harden much faster than when you work with joint compound.

Flared Box Planter

You may recognize the shape of this planter from the clock earlier in the book. That's because it is the same shape and pattern! It is easy to adapt foam décor projects for different uses. The crystal knob feet and lion's head detail are great touches for this garden setting.

Level 2

Safety First!

- **Use goggles and a fume mask when working with the heated knife.**
- **Be sure to sit the tool on a proper stand. It gets very hot!**
- **Use pliers to tighten the tip if it comes loose.**

1. This is the same box as the Flared Box Clock (page 49). Follow the directions for how to assemble the Flared Box Clock until it is time to cover the foam. Instead of inserting finials for legs, use the crystal knobs. *Optional: If you want to use the box to plant fresh materials, melt a drainage hole in the bottom of the box with a straight tip on the heated tool.*

2. Mix tile grout and additive instead of water as directed on the package. Cover the outside and bottom of the box. Do not get grout in the holes for the knobs. Spread the grout with a putty knife and your hands (wear gloves). Glue the crystal knobs to the bottom of the planter. Allow the box to harden overnight.

3. Apply a coat of Sage paint. Allow this to dry.

4. Glue the wood Lion's head to the front of the box.

5. Antique the surface of the box with a mixture of diluted paint. Mix one part Olive Green paint to one part glazing medium, then apply the glaze with a paintbrush. Add more green at the bottom of the box than the top. Immediately blot away excess paint with a paper towel to soften the edges. Rub green glaze into the wood piece and blot the excess.

6. Protect the paint on the box with the clear sealer. Let the sealer dry before planting.

Materials

- Craft foam sheet, ½" x 12" x 36"
- Tile grout or joint compound
- Acrylic paint, Italian Sage and Olive Green Dark*
- Glazing medium*
- Clear outdoor weatherproofing sealer
- 1" bristle brush
- 4 faux crystal drawer knobs (for legs)
- Hobby wood lion's head piece*
- Flat top straight pins
- 10mm ball tip pins
- Disposable gloves
- Paper towels
- Hot multi-tipped tool with knife blade and straight tip*
- Putty knife
- Rubber mallet or hammer
- Paper towels
- Heavy-duty glue*

* Used in this project: Beacon Hold the Foam!™ glue; Walnut Hollow Creative Versa-Tool and wood lion's head; Plaid Enterprises Folk Art® acrylic paint and Glazing Medium; Minwax Helmsman outdoor sealer; Walnut Hollow Classic Dimensions wood decoration; and Liquid Nails® for Heavy-Duty Construction glue.

Quick Tip

- You will only need a small package of grout. Look at the variety of colors available. If you find a color that is promising, try it. If you do not like it, just apply outdoor paint over it.
- You may cover the foam with joint compound! Just add basement waterproofing paint before painting the box green.

Variations

- Use floral foam to secure artificial plants such as the orchid shown.
- Add river rocks to hide the foam.

Fabulous Floor Fountain

Just try to find a fountain like this at an affordable price! Try adding a few goldfish to complete the look!

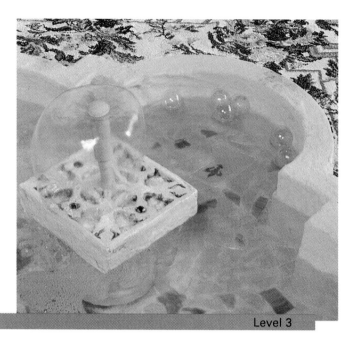

Level 3

Safety First!

- **Wear eye protection while working with a jigsaw.**
- **Always be aware of where your hands are when working with a jigsaw or any saw. Do not place fingers in front of the blade at any time.**
- **Wear a fume mask while mixing powdered grout and when using the heated tool.**

To make the basin:

1. Cut each round wreath in half. Be sure to cut straight through the foam.

2. Cut each square wreath into four equal pieces. Be sure to cut straight through each wreath.

3. Stack three circular wreath halves on top of one another. Glue them together with the construction glue. Repeat this step, and make three more stacks. Stack three of the square corners on top of one another and glue. Repeat this step to make four pointed corner stacks.

4. Lay out the pieces as shown in Fig. 9. If the edges do not meet flush, sand them. Glue the pieces together with construction glue. Reinforce the joints by inserting greening pins. From the outside, insert the pins so one half of the pin is in one layer, and the other half is in another layer. Allow the glue to cure for at least two hours.

5. After the pieces from Step 4 have dried, sit the glued basin sides Trace around the sides with the permanent marker. Make a mark on one side and another on the insulation foam. This will tell you where to line up the insulation foam later (because the sides will not end up being exactly the same on every side).

6. Remove the sides and cut out the traced shape for the bottom with a jigsaw (or coping saw). Dry fit the sides to the base. Reference your marks to start. If the bottom does not line up flush with the sides, make adjustments by sanding or cutting until it does.

7. Turn the sides upside down. Apply a generous bead of heavy-duty glue to the bottom of the wreath assembly. Add the bottom. Pin the bottom to the sides with several greening pins.

8. Have a friend help you turn the basin right side up. Apply caulk where all the layers of the basin meet. Let the caulk set up for 24 hours. Check the basin for leaks by adding water. Repair any leaks with additional caulk.

9. While the glue is curing, use the Ivory paint to spray the bell-pattern fountainhead, the shaft it attaches to, and the pump cord. Spray the parts lightly so as not to clog the fountainhead.

10. While the caulk cures, create the center plaque (see page 94).

11. After the caulk has cured for 24 hours, mix the grout to the package directions. Mix in the additive to make it weatherproof. Cover the inside on the sides first, then the bottom. Use a combination of the putty knife and your hands (wear the gloves). Place the decorative glass pieces (or tile) pieces on the bottom (while it is still wet) in a random pattern. Gently push each one so any sharp sides are covered with grout. Have fun and decorate the bottom as desired. I used iridescent glass pieces. *Tip: Be careful if you break your own glass pieces. They will be extremely sharp!*

12. Continue covering the rest of the basin with grout, mixing small batches at a time to prevent premature hardening!

Materials

To make the basin:
- 6 craft foam wreaths, 2" x 2" x 18"
- 3 square foam wreaths, 14" x 14"
- ½ sheet insulation foam, ½" thick
- Exterior spray paint, Hunter Green*
- Tile grout and acrylic additive, white
- Exterior latex paint, light green
- Caulking gun
- 3 to 4 tubes water-submersible caulk
- Plastic vase
- French Lace stencil*
- Mosaic glass pieces or tiles
- Greening pins
- Disposable gloves
- Jigsaw or coping saw
- Putty knife
- 3 to 4 tubes heavy-duty construction glue*
- Permanent marker
- Ruler
- Old bath towel

To make the center plaque:
- Craft foam sheet, ½" x 8" x 8"
- Craft foam sheet, 1" x 8" x 8"
- Small box unsanded grout, Almond
- Exterior spray paint, Ivory and Dark Brown*
- 20 or 30gph pond/fountain pump
- Decorative fountainhead (bell shape)
- 10mm length ball tip pins
- 4 marbles
- Flat head straight pins
- Hot multi-tipped tool with knife blade and straight tips*
- Shape cutter and self-healing mat*
- Bucket
- Trash bag or newspapers
- Mineral spirits
- Disposable gloves
- * Used in this project: Syndicate Sales plastic bowl; Walnut Hollow Creative Versa-Tool; StenSource® International stencil; Krylon Satin spray paint; Plaid Enterprises Folk Art® acrylic paint; and Liquid Nails® for Heavy-Duty Construction glue.

Variations

- Try a flexible rubber stamp if the spray-painted stencil is not a fun idea for you.
- Instead of green spray paint, purchase green outdoor craft paint.

Garden Gathering

- If grout sounds too diffi-cult, try applying joint compound to the foun-tain parts. After it is dried and sanded smooth, add three coats of basement waterproof-ing paint. Allow the paint to dry between coats. Once the basement paint is dry, add exterior paint in the colors of your choice. For the bottom mosaic, apply the pieces with clear adhesive, allow it to dry, and then use grout to fill in between the pieces.

- It is important to use a water-submersible caulk. Ask someone at a home store to help you find one, or you may get dizzy reading the numer-ous labels! If you are still unsure about your prod-uct, call the manufac-turer. They will help you find the correct product.

- For most outdoor proj-ects, I like to use tile grout because it is inex-pensive, quick, and does not require further waterproofing. Beware! The grout will harden much faster than joint compound. Purchase smaller boxes of grout to mix as needed.

- Grout now comes in a number of great colors. You may either purchase a grout that is pre-col-ored, or use a color additive. For this project, we just painted over the grout with exterior paint.

13. After the grout has cured, apply a coat of light green paint to the entire basin, including the bottom. Wipe the paint off the mosaic bottom as you go to prevent hiding the pieces. Allow the paint to dry.

14. Add the stenciling to the sides. Turn the basin on its side to work. Place a towel underneath to prevent chipping the grout. Place the sten-cil on one curved side of the fountain. Spray the stencil with the green paint. Press the stencil onto the curved surface as you move along the pattern. Your hands will get sprayed. Wear gloves. Continue around the basin until each curved side is stenciled.

To make the center plaque:

1. Use the shape cutter to cut out the black areas from the pattern.

2. Cut the 1" and ½" thick foam into 8" x 8" squares with the knife blade attached to the heated tool. For the 1" foam, you may only be able to score the 1" thick foam with the blade and then break off the excess. Sand the edges with a scrap piece of foam.

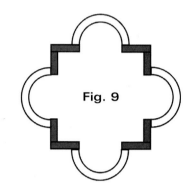

Fig. 9

3. Pin the pattern to the ½" square. Cut out all of the open areas with the heated tool. Use a straight tip on the tool to melt the circles. Once the foam is cut, place it on top of the other square. Melt a hole in the 1" thick square that is the same size as the piece on top of it.

4. Mix the Almond grout as directed on the package. Dip the uncut square into the grout. Place it on a trash bag or newspapers to dry. Place scrap pieces of foam or rocks under the square, so it does not stick to the drying surface.

5. Dip the ½" thick decorative piece into the grout. Place this piece directly on top of the other square. Line up the edges. Smooth the sides where the pieces meet. Let the pieces cure.

6. Apply a coat of Dark Brown paint to the square plaque. Immediately wipe away most of the paint with paper towels dipped in paint thinner (or mineral spirits). Wear gloves. Leave paint mostly in the recessed areas of the plaque. Insert marbles into the four indentations.

7. Using the heated tool (with the straight tip in it), turn the plastic vase upside down and melt a hole large enough for the pump shaft to fit through. Next, melt a hole for the pump cord to feed through so the vase will sit flat.

8. Attach the smaller shaft (for the decorative bell) to the pump. For now, leave off the larger piece that attaches to the top of the shaft. Place the pump motor in the center of the basin. Cover the motor with the upside down vase. Slide on the plaque. Add the decorative fountainhead (bell attachment). Make sure the plug on the cord is away from the water basin. Fill the basin with about four inches of water.

9. Once the water is added, plug in the fountain and marvel in its glory! If necessary, adjust the water flow on the fountain until the spray looks right. This fountain is sure to become the crowning glory of your garden or patio, and you did it yourself! Great job!

Tip: Never run the pump dry!

One more idea...

Gallery

Celtic motifs make gorgeous foam décor. You have already learned how to build a foam box, so go find an interesting Celtic pattern and carve it into the foam. Try something simple at first, such as the smaller box pictured, then go for the more intricate ones!

Foam panels are carved then assembled to create Celtic planters. The foam is great for outdoor fresh plantings because water will drain from the bottom of the box if it left uncovered.

Resources

Beacon Adhesives
(914) 699-3400
beaconadhesives@yahoo.com
Hold the Foam!™ glue and Foam Finish™

Benjamin Moore Paints
(800) 344-0400
info@benjaminmoore.com
www.benjaminmoore.com
Shenandoah Taupe and Hot Springs Stones paints

Design Master
www.dmcolor.com
Modern Metals Metallic Taupe paint

Dremel
(800) 437-3635
www.dremel.com
Multi-Pro rotary tool

Fiskars®
(800) 950-0203
www.fiskars.com
Acrylic ruler, Softouch™ scissors, Shape Cutter™, self-healing mat, paper edgers

Krylon
(800) 4-KRYLON
www.krylon.com
Make It Stone® spray paint, red primer paint

Jaquard
(800) 442-0455
www.jacquardproducts.com
Pearl Ex Powder

Minwax
(800) 523-9299
www.minwax.com
Dark walnut stain, Helmsman clear outdoor sealant, and Spar Urethane

Modern Options
(510) 614-3900
info@modernoptions.com
www.ModernOptions.com
Sophisticated Finishes Instant Iron and Instant Rust paints and clear sealer

Plaid Enterprises
(678) 291-8100
www.plaidonline.com
Folk Art® acrylic paint, glazing medium, Modge Podge®, antiquing medium, Eggshell crackle kit, Apple Barrel® paints, combing tool, outdoor gloss acrylic enamel, bottle-top paintbrush

Plastifoam® craft foam
Syndicate Sales, Inc.
(800) 428-0515
www.syndicatesales.com

StenSource® International
(800) 642-9293
generalinfo@stensource.com
www.stensource.com
Victorian Swirl stencil, French Lace stencil

STYROFOAM® brand craft foam
The Dow Chemical Company
www.stryofoam-chenille.com

Timeless Frames
(315) 782-3302
weloveframes@timelessframes.com
www.timelessframes.com
Collections shadow box

Valspar
(888) 313-5569
Millstone paint, Weathered Crackle paint

Walnut Hollow
(800) 950-5101
comments@walnuthollow.com
www.walnuthollow.com
Creative Versa-Tool™, Classic Dimensions hobby wood